FROM THE
A Guideb(

"This guidebook for writers is an absolute treat—with clean, lovely writing that draws you into vivid stories and meditations on family and on the natural world. Edge, a generous writer, weaves those stories—and illustrative poems—with writing advice that is both practical and reverent. As a writer and a reader, I came away inspired."
—**Lyn Millner, MFA**, Professor, Founder of Florida Gulf Coast University's Journalism Program, author of *The Allure of Immortality: An American Cult, a Florida Swamp, and a Renegade Prophet.*

"There's something for everyone in this mixed-genre guidebook for the writing life: short-short stories, poetry, essays on writing, and memoir. Throughout the book, Charlene Edge draws us into worlds both real and imagined, with the remarkable ability to capture the past in almost photographic detail. The selves in these pages absorb death and loss, contemplate religion in all its trappings, and find beauty and pathos in subjects ranging from the imagined life of earthly objects (an antique iron) to the stars ("rolling jewels in heaven's palm"). The spine that holds the stories and poems together is the series of short essays about writing that highlight Edge's creative process and offer useful advice on topics ranging from self-publishing to writing exercises." —**Rachel Newcomb, PhD**, Rollins College Professor of Anthropology, author of *The Gift*; *Women of Fez*; and *Encountering Morocco: Fieldwork and Cultural Understanding.*

"Charlene L. Edge writes from the intersection of love, life, and loss, and she does so in the front window, where readers and writers can see how she works her craft. I highly recommend this guidebook for writers." —**Susan Campbell, MS**, Pulitzer Prize-winning journalist, Distinguished Lecturer of Journalism, University of New Haven, author of *Dating Jesus: A Story of Fundamentalism, Feminism, and the American Girl,* and other books.

FROM THE
PORCH
TO THE
PAGE

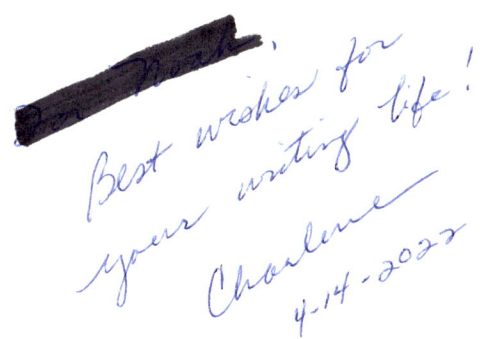

Best wishes for your writing life!
Charlene
4-14-2022

FROM THE
PORCH
TO THE
PAGE

A Guidebook for the Writing Life

Charlene L. Edge

NEW WINGS
PRESS, LLC

From the Porch to the Page: A Guidebook for the Writing Life. Copyright © 2022 by Charlene L. Edge. All rights reserved. Printed and bound in the United States of America.

This book is a collection of fiction, poetry, and nonfiction. Some names, characters, places, and incidents are either products of the author's imagination or are used fictitiously.

Cover and interior design by Duane Stapp

Cover image © GeniusMinus-stock.adobe.com

Cover author photo by Hoyt L. Edge

Author photo by Hoyt L. Edge

Library of Congress Control Number: 2022905437

No part of this book may be reproduced or transmitted in any form or by any means, electronic or mechanical, including photocopying, recording, or by an information storage and retrieval system—except by a reviewer who may quote brief passages in a review to be printed in a magazine, newspaper, or on the Web—without permission in writing from the publisher at New Wings Press, LLC.

Permission requests can be made by contacting the author at https://charleneedge.com/contact.

Because of the dynamic nature of the internet, any web addresses or links contained in this book may have changed since publication and may no longer be valid.

ISBN: 978-0-9978747-2-3

Published by New Wings Press, LLC
527 Henkel Circle
Winter Park, Florida 32789

For information about special discounts for bulk purchases, please send a request to the author at https://charleneedge.com/contact.

In loving memory of Ruth Mullen—activist, writer, and brilliant, good-humored copyeditor.
(JUNE 22, 1953–SEPTEMBER 7, 2021)

Acknowledgments

Grateful acknowledgment goes to the editors of the following publications in which these pieces in *From the Porch to the Page: A Guidebook for the Writing Life* originally appeared, sometimes in earlier versions.

The Florida Writer Magazine: "Nocturnal Impositions," "Melanie's Sign," "A Farmer Secret," "Off the Cliff: From Manuscript to Printed Book."

The Florida Palm Vol. 6, No. 4 Fall 2006: "Letter to the Editor." This poem was also read on Orlando, Florida's public radio station WM-FE-FM in a segment of *Poetic Logic* hosted by Sara Schlossman, April 25, 2003. It aired within *The Arts Connection* program produced by Becky Morgan.

The Rollins Book of Verse, 1885-2010: "He Was the Grounded Grass."

Wordsmith '97, Anthology of the Tampa Writers Alliance (TWA): "Chameleon One" and "A Shirt Not Her Own," which, under the title "A Bar Iron," won second prize in the TWA contest judged by Rita Ciresi.

Wordsmith '98, Anthology of the Tampa Writers Alliance (TWA): "From Hills Avenue" and "He Was the Grounded Grass," first prize winner in the TWA contest judged by Peter Meinke.

The *Florida Writers Association* website blog: short essays about writing, many in earlier versions.

ICSA Today Vol. 7, No. 2, 2016, 15-17: "Why I Had to Escape a Fundamentalist Cult." Reprinted with permission of the International Cultic Studies Association, P.O. Box 2265, Bonita Springs, FL 34133, Phone: 239.514.3081, Fax: 305.393.8193, e-mail: mail@icsamail.com, web: http://www.icsahome.com

Author's Note

Welcome to *From the Porch to the Page: A Guidebook for the Writing Life*. You may know my work because you've read posts on my website or journeyed with me through my award-winning memoir, *Undertow: My Escape from the Fundamentalism and Cult Control of The Way International*. New Wings Press, LLC. 2017.

Undertow, like an extra-wide semi-truck, dominated my writing life for many years, but it has turned a corner now, and the bicycles, cars, and taxis stuck behind it have revved up and are now moving forward on the road of this guidebook. They are poems and short-short stories to illustrate points made about writing in the short essays.

One essay, "Writing Behind the Scenes in Kas, Turkey," first appeared on my website, along with the photo of me on the cover of this book taken at the Hideaway Hotel in Kas, Turkey, 2011. Most of the remaining essays (some in earlier forms) were first published month by month on the Florida Writers Association website during 2017–2020. "Poetry in Solitude" under the title of "Writing Benefits in Solitude," published April 15, 2020, seemed relevant for angst-filled writers (like me) with heavy hearts overwhelmed by the COVID-19 pandemic, which, unfortunately, continues as I write this note.

The six short-short stories, sometimes called flash fiction or sudden fiction, feature adventures of a character named Melanie Craven, the star of this guidebook's centerpiece story "From the Porch," in "Part VI: Writing Stories," and again in "Part X: More Melanie Stories."

Some poems you find sprinkled throughout the book originate from my writing life in Tampa, Florida, during the mid-1990s, while others began later at Rollins College in a nurturing writers' group called "First Friday." I mention this because it's easy to forget that all of our writing, no matter its age, imprints our creative body of work.

Whether or not you are a writer, I hope you enjoy reading this book. It's a genuine honor to offer it. Pour yourself a cup of coffee (or a glass of wine), pull up a chair, and mull over what you find here.

Charlene Edge
Winter Park, Florida
December 23, 2021

Gratitude

I am profoundly indebted to my generous writer-friends who sharpened up different pieces and parts of this guidebook: Robyn Allers, Stacey Boo, Nylda Dieppa, Virginia Higgins, Karl Kahler, Janne Lane, Sara Schlossman, and Maureen Townsend. I am humbled by their devoted interest in my writing and their love for me. I also thank my dear daughter and son-in-law, Rachel and Adam Chase, for their enthusiastic feedback, as well as Mary Ann de Stefano, Editor, *The Florida Writer* magazine, for her nourishing belief in my work.

I'm forever grateful to the writing teachers and poets who've guided my work and inspired me to keep at it, including: Linda Goddard, MA, Russ Kesler, Lezlie Laws, PhD, Dionisio D. Martinez, the late Philip F. Deaver, EdD, and the late Mary Elizabeth "Bettie" Perez. Special thanks go to the faculty of the English Department at Rollins College—a liberal arts college—during my studies there (1990-1994), and for the student internship Rollins awarded me at *Orlando Magazine*, where I learned a bit of journalism.

For this book, I'm thrilled to work again with professionals vital to making my memoir, *Undertow*, an award-winning book: Alice Peck, book editor, whose writing wisdom is a beautiful gift; her expertise is my safe haven. Duane Stapp, book designer, who again produced a spot-on cover and lovely interior design. And a special thanks goes to Crystal Sershen, an outstanding copy and line editor, who stepped in after the tragic death of our friend, Ruth Mullen, copyeditor for *Undertow*, to whom I dedicate this book. May she rest in peace.

My deepest gratitude goes to my patient husband, Rollins College Professor Emeritus of Philosophy Hoyt L. Edge, PhD, whose faithful care, thoughtful first-reader comments, and love beyond measure help me grow and enjoy my writing life.

Table of Contents

Preface 1

I   READERS BECOME WRITERS   7

    Do Writers Have a Sacred Duty? 9
    Gifts, Apples, Fence 12

II   GETTING STARTED   15

    Writing the Truth 17
    Poem: Rosary 22
    Poem: Eclipse 24
    Writing Advice from Running Track 25
    Poem: Still 28
    Be Still and Receive 29
    Poem: In View 31
    Write by Hand or Keyboard? 33
    What's on Your Writing Desk 36
    Poem: In Magnification 38
    Unblock Writer's Block 39
    📖 A Book I Recommend About
    Unlocking Creativity 41

Camera-Eyes: A Writing Prompt 42

Poem: A Shirt Not Her Own 44

III WORDS BECOME SENTENCES   45

Vocabulary, Mysteries, and Prevarication 47

Building Great Sentences 50

📖 Books I Recommend about Sentences 52

Word Jumble Game 53

Dr. Metaphor and Tadpole 55

Poem: He Was the Grounded Grass 58

Poem: Past   Now   Future 59

Diction: Desire Pickiness 60

Poem: Dust 64

Tighten Up: Cut the Clichés 65

Nothing Like a Smooth Transition 68

IV WRITING MEMOIR   73

Poem: Christine 75

Memoir: Whose Story Is It Anyway? 76

📖 Books I Recommend That Help Me
Be a Better Writer 80

📖 Books I Recommend Specifically
on Writing Memoir 81

Poem: False Moves 82

Differences Between Memoir
and Autobiography 84

Why I Had to Escape a
Fundamentalist Cult 87

V WRITING POEMS   97

Poem: The First 99

Poetry and Solitude 102
   📖 Books I Recommend for
Writing Poetry 104
Poems: More of Charlene's Poems 105

VI WRITING STORIES   115

Writing a Very Short Story 117
   📖 Books I Recommend for
Writing Stories 119
"From the Porch" (a Short-Short Story) 120
Poem: Chameleon One 126

VII TRAVEL WRITING   127

Poem: With Dragons 129
Writing Meaningful Travel Stories 130
   📖 Books I Recommend for
Travel Writing 133
Poem: Gadfly 134
Writing Behind the Scenes in Kas, Turkey 135

VIII KEEP MOVING/INSPIRATION   139

Poem: Letter to the Editors 141
Writing a Moment of Being 143
Cut Loose: Walk, Think, Write 146
Poem: Arrangements 149
   📖 Reading I Recommend about Walking ... 150
So WHAT? Writing Here Alone Together 151
Is This Your Season to Keep Writing? 154
Experiment with Writing Prompts 156
   📖 Books I Recommend for Finding
Writing Prompts 158

What's Your Writer-Context? 159
Velcro Moments—Making Your
Writing Stick 163
Nudge Reports: Making Impossible Dreams
Come True 167
The End: Are We There Yet? 171
Poem: From Hills Avenue 174

IX   IT'S A BOOK, NOW WHAT?   175

Off the Cliff: From Manuscript
to Printed Book 177
📖 A Book I Recommend for Writers
Seeking Publishers 179
Mini-Marketing for Maxi-Messages 180

X   MORE MELANIE STORIES   185

Let Father In 187
Melanie's Sign 193
Nocturnal Impositions 196
B Is for Baby Names 199
A Farmer Secret 202

XI   IF YOU WANT TO KEEP WRITING   205

A Writer's D-List 207

Appendix 1 – Timeline for Writing &
Self-Publishing *Undertow* 217

Appendix 2 – Mini-Marketing Flyer 223

Selected Bibliography 225

About the Author 231

INDEX to Charlene's Poems

Rosary	22
Eclipse	24
Still	28
In View	31
In Magnification	38
A Shirt Not Her Own	44
He Was the Grounded Grass	58
Past Now Future	59
Dust	64
Christine	75
False Moves	82
The First	99
Migration	105
In Secret	106
Matches	107
Chowchilla, California: July 15, 1976	108
Tears	110
Fly, Woman-Child, Fly	111
Encounters	113
Chameleon One	126
With Dragons	129
Gadfly	134
Letter to the Editors	141
Arrangements	149
From Hills Avenue	174

Preface

Besides the satisfaction of seeing our words published, what other basic characteristic might writers have in common? Hint: it makes publication possible. Annie Dillard lays it out for us in her book *The Writing Life*, when she relays an anecdote of a fellow writer who had a student who asked, "Do you think I could be a writer?"

"Well," the writer said, "do you like sentences?"

We don't find out what the student thought or did after that answer, but let's hope the message hit its mark. Dillard reframes the lesson: "If you like sentences, then you can begin to write."

Notice she says, *begin*.

Makes sense. If I wondered whether I could be a painter but abhorred the stink of fresh paint on my brush, on the canvas, or on my pristine painting smock, then I'll bet you a dozen tubes of Winsor & Newton Winton 200-Milliliter Oil Paint—any color—that I wouldn't last long at the easel.

Sentences, NOT Words?

Notice in the anecdote what the writer/teacher did *not* say. She did *not* ask, "Do you like *words*?" Instead, she deliberately posited *sentences* as THE THING a wannabe writer needs to like. True, words fascinate, irritate, and congregate. Writers cannot live without them. So, why not say *words*—not *sentences*—are what writers need to like? I'll let professor, author, and columnist, Stanley Fish, answer from his book *How to Write a Sentence: And How to Read One.*

> ...while you can brush or even drip paint on canvas and make something interesting happen, just piling up words, one after the other, won't do much of anything until something else has been added. That something is named quite precisely by Anthony Burgess in this sentence from his novel *Enderby Outside* (1968): "And the words slide into the slots ordained by syntax, and glitter as with atmospheric dust with those impurities which we call meaning."

To put it another way, constructing sentences is not haphazard. If we're doing our job, good sentences appear thanks to one deliberate choice after another. Words placed in a certain order—known as *syntax*—create a specific meaning. And let's not fool around with meaning. Mis-conveyed meanings can cause [insert a disaster of your choice here].

Nestled in Their Nests
Fish continues:

> Before the words slide into their slots, they are just discrete items, pointing everywhere and anywhere.... Once the words are nestled in the places "ordained" for them ... they are subjects or objects or actions or descriptives or indications of manner, and as such they combine into a statement about the world, that is, into a meaning that one can contemplate, admire, reject, or refine.

I love words *nestled* in places perfect for them in the sentence, like baby birds snug in the nest their momma bird created. Isn't that integral to the joy we feel in writing a good sentence—we find a noun, adjective, or verb that we really want to use and arrange other words around it to create an intended effect? Or we write a noun-verb kind of sentence and then experiment with adjectives to describe the noun we used. Here's a smashing sentence from one of my favorite authors, Michael Ondaatje, poet and novelist, from his masterpiece, *The English Patient*, which won the Booker Prize.

> The desert could not be claimed or owned—it was a piece of cloth carried by winds, never held down by stones, and given a hundred shifting names long before Canterbury existed, long before battles and treaties quilted Europe and the East.

I think that verb "quilted" is pure genius. Ondaatje brings to mind what many craftspeople do: they sew many small, diverse fabric remnants together to create one large coverlet called a quilt. By using the verb quilted, Ondaatje's point is swiftly made about the goal of battles and treaties, only they do it with lands and nations.

What about *Liking* Sentences?

As writers, we sometimes find ourselves spending way more time with sentences than anything else—reading them and writing them. So, as with people, if you're going to hang around with sentences for hours on end, it helps if you like them. Yes?

Yes, but I say we need more. I think whoever aspires to write seriously and with purpose cannot persist with simply *liking* sentences. To continue this daunting work that exhilarates us, I think we must love and *stay in love* with sentences. After all, doesn't *love* exceed *like*? Love, not *like*, changes the stinky adjective at 2:00 a.m. When love receives tough criticism, it takes it on the chin. Even if the only option is writing on paper towels, love will revise the last paragraph over and over and over. I say a better answer to the question, "Do you think I could be a writer?" is "Do you absolutely *love* sentences?" Love is what enlivens, motivates, and sustains the writing. And it does the same for writers.

Writers do not merely reflect and interpret life; they inform and shape life.
—E. B. White, *The Paris Review Interviews, IV*

I
READERS BECOME WRITERS

Do Writers Have a Sacred Duty?

In 1988, at thirty-six, I took my first full-blown creative writing class at what was called, during those years, Valencia Community College in Orlando, Florida. The first night of class, our teacher rushed into the room, muttered a brief hello, and launched into the session this way: "Let's start with the basics. First, what is the writer's sacred duty?" He peered at students in the front row. "Writers, speak up!" Bushy eyebrows bouncing up and down, he gripped the small brown lectern. I panicked. I'd recently returned to college after more than a decade, unsure of myself as a student, and much less sure of having the title "writer." I just wanted to fulfill a college requirement with this class, not become a novelist. Furthermore, writers being bound to any duty, sacred or otherwise, was news to me.

"Write every day," somebody offered.

"Nope." Our teacher craned his neck, sized us up, inspected our body language. "Next?"

"We should submit our stories for publication ... and not give up," said the guy in front of me.

"That's great, but ... anyone else?" Our teacher's shoulders slumped. He sighed and pointed to a woman in the back row.

"Be part of a writers' critique group." As several of us turned around to look at her, her face turned as pink as the sweater she wore. "You know ... to get feedback and improve?"

"A good idea for sure, but not a writer's non-negotiable, unavoidable responsibility. Hint: it is right under our noses." I looked away from our teacher and down at my desk. He leaned over the podium. "Read."

A collective moan rolled through the room. Thanks to our teacher's engaging approach, our embarrassment at overlooking the obvious melted away. Of course, we had to read. We wanted to read. We loved to read. At least I did. But I had not yet realized the *essential* building block that reading is to the ability to write well.

"You all knew that, right?" he laughed and flashed his captivating grin. "First and foremost, we are readers of literature," he emphasized *readers*. "Reading is the writer's one and only holy duty." Then he added this important point: he didn't mean we should read only books about *how* to write, although they help. He meant we needed to study stories, novels, poems, and plays written by accomplished authors who know what they're doing on the page. Reading a variety of authors' voices gives us a multitude of ways to absorb cadence, pace, the ins and outs of sentences, the music of it all.

As examples, he pointed out how musicality echoes in great Russian novels, as well as in the prose of Henry James, William Faulkner, Margaret Atwood, Alice Munro—masters every single one.

What's on Your Sacred-Duty List?

In her forceful book *The Writing Life*, Annie Dillard points out:

> The writer studies literature, not the world. He lives in the world; he cannot miss it. If he has ever bought a hamburger, or taken a commercial airplane flight, he spares his readers a report of his experience [unless he is a travel writer]. He is careful of what he reads, for that is what he will write. He is careful of what he learns, because that is what he will know.

Dillard cautions us to be careful of what we read and learn. We should ask ourselves about the quality of the books we read. If we always eat junk food, we pay a high price health-wise. Same goes for reading and writing. One way I found to add vitamins to my sacred-duty diet is to meet regularly with some friends in a book club. We read a range of novels, memoirs, and other nonfiction books, short stories, even meaty magazine articles. As I read them, I try to notice how authors structure their stories, write dialogue, produce a rhythm of sentences. I like to sit back, sink into the writing of outstanding authors, like this mesmerizing passage from Margaret Atwood's *The Handmaid's Tale*:

> There was old sex in the room and loneliness, and expectation, of something without a shape or name. I remember that yearning, for something that was always about to happen and was never the same as the hands that were on us there and then, in the small of the back, or out back, in the parking lot, or in the television room with the sound turned down and only the pictures flickering over lifting flesh.

This paragraph by Atwood nourishes my writing spirit with its well-done innuendos. I love the way she captures the tense, creepy atmosphere of the horrible situation without making me want to shut the book.

What's next on your sacred-duty list?

Gift, Apples, Fence

On January 22, 1999, I attended a writerly event at the University of Central Florida: "Distinguished Author Series: Margaret Atwood." Yes, THE famous Margaret Atwood. You may know that Atwood, a Canadian, authored the best-selling, horrifying, dystopian novel *The Handmaid's Tale* (1985), which television producers—with their sights on America's inflamed neurosis about the workings of cults—fed into the airwaves as a television series for all the world to watch.

But in 1999, when I stood in the aisle to see Atwood in the overcrowded UCF auditorium, it wasn't Atwood's discussion of her terrifying novel, along with other work, that made the biggest impression on me. It wasn't even her reputation as one of the finest living writers. No, it was someone else's book she acclaimed as a "must read" for writers, painters, playwrights, and poets, and what we call "the general public." It's a little book that stirs up a big subject—*The Gift: Imagination and the Erotic Life of Property* by Lewis Hyde.

Hyde's book cover intrigues me. It draws us into the story with the reproduction of a piece of art titled *Basket of Apples*. On the copyright page, we discover this: the art is reprinted through the courtesy of the Shaker Community, Inc., a faith community that flourished in the northeast US during the 1700s and 1800s in which members shared their lives and goods. I learned from Wikipedia that even though men and women usually labored separately on the commune, they did unite to harvest something nourishing: rosy-colored apples.

What's So Great about *The Gift*?

The dedication page says it all. "What is good is given back." As writers, what we have is a gift. We express what's inside of us (a gift) with words that appear outside of us. We give of the gift we have. On the first pages of the book's introduction, Hyde lets us know what he thinks about this.

> It is the assumption of this book that a work of art is a gift, not a commodity. Or, to state the modern case with more precision, that works of art exist simultaneously in two "economies," a market economy and a gift economy. Only one of those is essential, however: a work of art can survive without the market, but where there is no gift there is no art.

One Way to Read *The Gift*

Start at the end. Begin with the conclusion of *The Gift*. It is about ten pages long. One incident Hyde offers is a story told by the Chilean poet, Pablo Neruda. When Neruda was a child, he received a toy from a child he didn't see, who stuck his hand through a hole in their shared backyard fence and gave him a "marvelous white toy sheep." During those moments, neither child spoke. To give back, out of gratitude, in the spirit of sharing, Pablo ran in the house, returned, and put his favorite toy through that same hole, "a pine cone, opened, full of odor and resin, which I adored." Give your writing gifts the best nourishment, attention, and expression you can. You never know who may receive your gift. And just like the anonymous child on the other side of that fence, you'll likely never meet most of your readers.

II

GETTING STARTED

Writing the Truth

No matter what awful situation surrounds us, as writers, we know a secret that can rid us of the blues. What is it? On the nearest blank page, write whatever comes to your mind. And keep writing. Write what you *really* feel, smell, see, hear, and touch. No one is watching. You're free to lose yourself in some messy sentences, brainstorm new characters, or experiment with adjectives you rarely use, like "cumulative" to describe sentences that build to a crescendo.

In your journal, which no one should ever read without permission, write the truth about what bothers you, what helps you. Scribble whatever comes into your mind and do *not* stop for fifteen minutes. Or look out the window and daydream awhile. The daydreams and stray thoughts that come through your mind are all part of truth-telling work.

Inspiration Begets Inspiration

One year during the holidays, my husband and I visited some of his cousins, their adult children, and their grandchildren, who ran around the house laughing while we adults stood around the periphery talking. One adult-child-of-a-cousin and I found ourselves talking about writing. She wore not only a shining smile on her face, but bright red writing anxiety on her sleeve. As she continued rambling about writing—its slow starts, false starts, and shitty first drafts—I tried to help her brush off some of her blank-page fear. For a few minutes, we commiserated about sitting down to make words real on paper rather than letting them float like fog in our minds. Then something surprising happened ... well, maybe not all that surprising. As it often does, in offering good cheer, some good cheer came back to me.

My Favorite Book about Writing

I told her about a book on the writing life / writing craft that I fell in love with years ago. It comforts me, boosts my confidence, and touches my heart deep inside. It was not preachy or intimidating, just a little book—only 179 pages—that contains significant wisdom. It was written by the funny, dedicated, and inspired writing teacher, Brenda Ueland (1891-1985). Here's a bit from *Goodreads* (a website) about Ueland and the liberating book she wrote.

> Brenda Ueland was a journalist, editor, freelance writer, and teacher of writing. She is best known for her book *If You Want to Write: A Book about Art, Independence and Spirit [1938]*.... She attended Wells and Barnard colleges and received her baccalaureate from Barnard in 1913. She lived in and around New York City for much of her adult life before returning to Minnesota in 1930.... Ueland would spend her life as a staunch feminist and is said to have lived by two rules: To tell the truth, and to not do anything you don't want to.

Telling the Truth

Tell the truth. My relative and I reflected on telling the truth, especially in a memoir. When you disclose truth in your nonfiction story, someone may surely get hurt. For sound advice on that topic, I recommend Judith Barrington's *Writing the Memoir: From Truth to Art*. The cover says it is "a practical guide to the craft, the personal challenges, and ethical dilemmas of writing your true stories." Inside the book, Barrington tells us:

> To write honestly about our lives requires that we work at

and refine our artistic skills so that our memoirs can effectively communicate our hard-won, deep layers of truth that are rarely part of conventional social discourse.

Memoir writing often encompasses pulling back curtains to reveal a complicated mess, so I suggest we learn how to write memoir with grace and honesty as best we can. You may find other helpful books, too, but Barrington's helped me the most.

But wait, there's more! We do not limit writing truth to the genre of memoir or other types of nonfiction. In any fiction or poetry, or any other genre, Ueland urges us to tell the truth about what we see and feel; about what our characters see and feel. Whatever we write, readers can sense whether or not it is the truth. Describe people, events, and emotions with care. Cut clichés. Take courage. Convey each line with all the love and concentration you can.

Ueland fills the pages of her wonderful book with stories about her students as they shed fear and trepidation (and sometimes laziness and pretentiousness) to write with energy and truth. Here's an example:

> A girl in my class once described a young man, her hero, by saying, "His muscles rippled through his shoulders."
>
> I turned to her and said, "Are you sure they really rippled? They so often ripple in fiction, but have you seen that? Can you see this young man clearly in your imagination? Can you tell me what he looked like?"
>
> She said very earnestly, "Yes I can. And they did ripple. His shoulders were very big and looked as if they would burst through the seams in his coat."
>
> "Well," I said, "put that down. That is just wonderful, a fine graphic description."

To get original work on the page, Ueland reminded her students that they only needed to do one thing: tell the truth.

Everybody is original, if he tells the truth, if he speaks from himself. But it must be from his *true* self and not from the self he thinks he *should* be. Jennings at Johns Hopkins, who knows more about heredity and the genes and chromosomes than any man in the world, says that no individual is exactly like any other individual, that no two identical persons have ever existed. Consequently, if you speak or write from *yourself* you cannot help being original.

We are each original. No one else can do our writing for us; no one else can tell our truth—or create our beautiful work. Remember poet John Keats's famous praise of truth and its association to beauty.

Consider this:

In the last two lines of "Ode on a Grecian Urn," the urn "speaks," and Keats sums up the message of this timeless work of art as:

"Beauty is truth, truth beauty,—that is all
Ye know on earth, and all ye need to know."

In other words, beauty is all we need in order to discover truth, and truth is itself beautiful. This is all we, mere mortals, know, but it's all we need to know: we shouldn't impatiently go in pursuit of answers which we don't need to have. Implied in these last lines of Keats's poem is the suggestion that we shouldn't attempt to find concrete answers to everything; sometimes the mystery is enough.[1]

Lastly, let me offer one of my favorite quotes on this subject. I even memorized it years ago, and it's been there for me in many moments of doubt. It's from *Hamlet*, by our old friend William Shakespeare,

---

[1] Visit the website: https://interestingliterature.com/2021/06/keats-beauty-is-truth-truth-beauty-meaning-analysis.

who put this wisdom in the mouth of Polonius: "To thine own self be true, and it must follow, as the night the day, thou canst not then be false to any man."

Be brave. Write the truth. Write something beautiful.
Write on and on.

Rosary

For my mother, Anne R. Lamy
June 8, 1920–November 27, 1968

One last look. They sit me in a chair,
one instant between me and her cold metal bed.
Across the room, her rosary hangs: a ring of rosebuds for the counting.
A saint's relic plays the guard, unshamed by
impotence.
Thick silence pounds in and out. My wool coat thin,
useless. All the mittens in the world cannot warm me now.

Leaves of Grass, Dali's whims, Jesuit anointings
fed her spirit, that,
after years in muffled rooms
now wrestles free of scowling healers
with frayed empty faces—
my mother's disconnection shutters against all of it.

One last look. Her waxen face mirrors
empty eyes of stained-glass saints.
Holy Mary, Mother of God,
her voice comes through my memory,
cold cloths she placed on my head,
sick and nursed, again and again.

Me in my virgin shoes cries, "Let's go back
to Rehoboth for one more swim," where
she tried to make sweet memories of goodbye.
But numbness comes like stiff iced air the day
we carved deep soft snow with angel wings,
touching, linked like rosary beads.

One last look. My chest frozen against,
"I'm so sorry about your mother."
I bit through chocolate-covered raisins
hidden in her dresser drawer, my fingers
fumbled through green plastic curlers,
searched for one last strand of hair.

Eclipse

At the stoplight, a Jaguar eclipsed us:
the homeless man on the bench
and me in my Sunbird Pontiac on my way home.

The driver looked dead ahead and straightened his tie.
I looked past the driver, through his car window,
and watched the homeless man on the bench.

His hair hung in strings,
His brown clothes wrinkled around him.
I watched him stare at the road.

Every day I drove past him,
he in a slump on the bench,
me in a slump at the wheel.

Today, like every other, I wondered how he got there.
I never once met his eyes,
although I was close enough for him to see my face.

But he never looked. He stared at the road,
as oblivious of me as I pretended to be of him
in my life away from the stoplight by his bench.

The man in the Jaguar sped away.
I drove home and shut the door.

Writing Advice from Running Track

Are you overwhelmed as I often am by the swirl of writerly information? Where have you discovered sound writing advice? The best advice I ever received was *not* from a writer-focused resource. In tenth grade at James M. Bennett Sr. High, I joined our school's first women's track team and learned an important lesson about writing.

Mrs. Baker (not her real name), our physical education teacher, inspired enough of us female wannabe track stars to make up a real team. Heady with excitement, we were proud to be "the first." Giddy, we'd stand around in our royal blue gym uniforms, spring wind blowing our ponytails, the tangy smell of mown grass wafting from the infield. Such novices! Most of us did not own real athletic shoes; I ran in Keds. In small-town USA during the late 1960s, we didn't know (or have) better. Nor did we know much about this sport. I liked to run, but had a lot of questions. How do you leap over those rickety hurdles? What about the relay race? If you cannot look back, how do you grab—and not drop—a baton from the runner behind you? When and how do runners breathe? What do you do if you trip or fall?

Don't Jump the Gun
Mrs. Baker was gentle; she encouraged us and made sure we listened. Her motto was, "Don't jump the gun." Because I was nervous, wanted to win, and thought I knew what to do, I anticipated the starting pistol firing before it did. *Bang!* I was already down the track. Come back. Start over. Pay attention. Run when it is time.

Hint to writers: don't jump the "get published" gun before your work is ready.

Get Good Coaches

Maybe you've watched hurdle jumpers at the Olympics on television. I was never *that* good, but wise Mrs. Baker recognized my determination to run the hurdles and asked the star hurdler on the men's track team to coach me. Patient and instructive, he became my hurdle brother. He made sure I practiced after school, no matter the weather. With care, he demonstrated how to keep my back leg bent in the proper position, at the perfect angle, so my toe didn't drop while I leapt over the hurdle. When your toe even *slightly* grazes the crossbar of the hurdle, down you go … your face in the track.

That spring, we competed against one of the few high school women's track teams in the area. Kelly-green infield grass and parents who cheered us onward filled my peripheral vision. Ahead of me lay white lines that divided gray lanes where hurdles, placed in regulated increments, resembled dominoes marching into the distance. The starting pistol fired. We leapt out of the blocks. Focused straight ahead, I cleared one, two, three hurdles. Then it happened. The number of steps I needed between each hurdle got thrown off; I shuffled to adjust, but my legs did not react fast enough. I don't know if the phrase "off-track" originates from track-team jargon, but I do know I got out of step and went ever-so-slightly out of my lane. That was my downfall. Literally. My back knee dropped too low, my toe caught the hurdle, and I hit the ground.

Get Up and Go

I was more embarrassed than hurt. Sprawled on the dusty track, my face aflame, I shut down. I heard nothing around me, even though I'm sure people called out from the sidelines (they later told me so). What I did hear were voices inside me: my parents', my coach's, my hurdle brother's, that formed a chorus: "Get up. Keep going, Charlene. Just finish!"

With eyes down, I wanted to disappear into the crowd, but those inner voices persisted. I hauled myself up, rubbed my burning knees, and limped down my lane toward the yellow finish tape, askew and limp on the track. I stepped over it. Our team had bonded well that spring, and my teammates patted my back in forgiveness. My coaches were good sports, too, pleased I hadn't run off in tears.

The rest of that season is a blurred memory of chilly afternoon practices and sore calf muscles. I can't remember whether I came in first or second or third place at any other track meet. But that's okay. Sometimes failures, more than successes, teach you lessons you need the most. The inner chorus, "Get up. Keep going. Just finish!" was not only the best track advice I ever got, it is the best writing advice I ever got … and can ever give. I stare down those hurdles on every page. Don't you?

Still

Be still, my lips, let my mind speak now.
Be still, my hands, so I can feel the peace I cannot touch
but touches me when I am still enough.

Be Still and Receive

"Great ideas fly through the universe all the time. Stand still long enough and one of them will hit you."

That was Isaac Asimov's answer to the question of where he got his fantastic story ideas. At least that is what fellow science fiction writer Ben Bova said of Asimov, scientist and famed author of nearly 500 books, many in the genre of science fiction.

Of course, the universe is rife with great ideas. But to catch a great idea, Asimov said, a person must be still.

My Dad and Asimov

When I was a kid, Asimov's novels lay scattered around our house. My father would settle in his black Naugahyde chair, a lamp sending light over his shoulder, and plunge into a paperback with Asimov's name on the cover. I never asked Dad what he liked about those stories, but perhaps he felt a kinship with Asimov's imagination. Asimov (1920-1992) and my father (1912-1997) were contemporaries, and both were scientists. My father was chief scientist at our county's Public Health Department; as a microbiologist, he looked through microscopes day after day. He spent hours in stillness.

Sometimes, when I visited my father at his laboratory, he'd let me peer through high-powered lenses to witness the movement of otherwise invisible life. I saw purple-stained amoebas, green squiggles, and reddish bits of life moving on their own. These life forms, which science made it possible for me to see, remind me to be still long enough to let an idea hit me—perhaps a children's story about a lavender amoeba?

Stillness Required

To see microscopic life, stillness is required. Isn't stillness also essential for writing? Those after-school be-still lessons in the laboratory likely swirl around in the background of my writing consciousness today, and they show up in the poem "In View," that follows this essay.

I remember another set of lenses Dad acquainted me with: our large telescope. If a solar or lunar eclipse was on its way, or just for the fun of it, Dad set the telescope on the front lawn, and it would transport us to another place. He showed me how to adjust those cumbersome lenses and focus on what he described as Orion, the Big and Little Dipper, or Venus, Saturn, or Mars. For those hours, we traveled across eons of time and space to the twinkling lights in the black distance, imagining what was out there.

Catching Ideas

Flash forward to 1995 when I heard Ben Bova pass along Asimov's advice at a Space Coast Writers Conference in Cocoa Beach, Florida. I sat enraptured by his talk of stories spun around scientific facts, other worlds, stars, planets, and moons. I recalled my father's love of science, that he read Asimov's books, and how he introduced me to tiny amoebas and mysterious planets. He showed me that to capture the riches of science, I had to settle down. Bova's second-hand encouragement from Asimov—be still to receive ideas flying through the universe—may now be third-hand advice, but it remains first-class wisdom.

In View

For my father, Joseph A. Lamy
February 9, 1912–July 4, 1997

At night near pine boughs my father
Would stand in our front yard,
search measureless heavens
with moonlit eyes.

He'd lower our telescope, steady on its tripod,
and with his sight settled in the instrument's cup,
he would turn and say,

"Here, be still and watch the moon,"
or "Can you spot the Little Dipper?"
simple forms for me at eight years old.
On tiptoes, I'd search through the magical lens.

By day, my father examined tiny creatures
alive in glass dishes, he peered through microscopes
at purple-stained amoebas teaching him
by shape, color, and movement
who they were within their cryptic spheres.

He would turn again and say,

"Here, be still and watch the paramecia,"
big word by then familiar to little me.
"… see them swim and dodge each other?"
On tiptoes again, I'd search through a lens—enchanted.

I think of you today, Dad, among
those rolling jewels in heaven's palm,
amid treasures shared on summer nights,
as side by side, we stood and met them.

Write by Hand or Keyboard?

Do you write by hand in a journal or notebook? Do you compose first drafts on yellow legal pads? Does your desk hold pens and pencils crammed into coffee cups, into spinning organizers, or jumbled in drawers? If you answered *yes* to any of the above, it's a sure bet you like to create the old-fashioned way: with a pen or pencil, in your unique penmanship, writing one word after another. You let words flow from your mind down through the pen as your hand travels slowly across the page; this expresses a heart-to-word connection. Longhand is about physicality, about the movement of your arm and hand and fingers to express your innermost thoughts and emotions.

Experiment: Compose by Hand Versus Keyboard

What you write with is a personal decision, but try an experiment. Leave your comfort zone and switch your method for a week to experience what happens. If you write by hand, use your computer (or typewriter if you still have one). Or if you type on the keyboard, dig out a pen or pencil you especially like. I use a sleek ballpoint pen whose weight feels comfortable in my fingers, whose point doesn't scratch against the paper but flows the ink smoothly onto the page.

Give yourself a couple of days and then assess. Do you notice any difference about the process, physically and/or mentally? How is the writing's flow? Do you sense more freedom to make a mistake and continue despite it, or do you edit on the spot more often than you do when writing your usual way? Do you second-guess yourself more about what shows up on the computer screen (or typewritten page) or in your handwriting on paper?

Body Language / Written Language

Let's consider how *body* language affects *written* language.

In her article, "Is It Better to Write by Hand or Computer?" published on the *Psychology Today* website (October 2, 2017), author Laura Deutsch clues us in:

> Many studies suggest that there are brain-friendly benefits of writing out letters, notes, essays, or journal entries by hand that you can't get from typing....
>
> Writing by hand connects you with the words and allows your brain to focus on them, understand them and learn from them. Other studies suggest that writing longhand is a workout for your brain. According to a *Wall Street Journal* article, some physicians claim that the act of writing—which engages your motor-skills, memory and more—is a good cognitive exercise for baby boomers who want to keep their minds sharp as they age. (See website, *Mental Floss*). Writing by hand helps people remember information and thus retain their memories as they age.

The Writer, the Words, the Point

Compared with ancient writers, such as the philosopher Aristotle and the poet Sappho, and more recent authors like Jane Austen and later, Franz Kafka, we may be fortunate to have more writing instruments to select from and to use at different stages in our process. Or maybe these choices postpone or weaken the writing. Who can say for sure? For some writers, it may be best to launch a story on paper and finish it there. Others may type the entire manuscript on the computer, revising along the way until the end. Some may switch around and combine methods.

Just remember: we're not always at the keyboard when we're compelled to write. For ideas that hit you on the run (or in bed after lights are out), jot them down by hand in a notebook; you may forget them if you don't. Next to my bed, I keep a little notebook and a pen that lights up after you click it twice. What an ingenious invention.

Eventually, though, if we plan to *publish* our work, even the most diehard hand-writers will have to face a computer and produce a digital copy. That facilitates sending it to first readers to get their feedback critique, and later to editors you may hire and publishers to whom you submit.

Whichever way(s) we use to get the words out, we shall keep on writing, keep on working. That is, of course, more important than our methods. That is, of course, the writer's point.

What's on Your Writing Desk?

Do you have a favorite quote or inspirational message in view as you write? How about scraps of paper with words of encouragement taped to your desk? I have a few of these; some old, some new. I love them. I need them. I keep them in plain sight to feed my soul, calm my mind, and keep my fingers moving words into view.

A Few of My Favorite Things
Here are a few bits within reading distance of my computer. Some are thumbtacked to the bulletin board on the wall above my computer monitor, others appear on small papers taped to different levels of my desk. Over time, edges of the papers have curled and yellowed, but the power of their messages has neither faded nor failed me.

1. "But the writer who endures and keeps working will finally know that writing the book was something hard and glorious, for at the desk a writer must try to be free of prejudice, meanness of spirit, pettiness and hatred, strive to be a better human being than the writer normally is, and to do this through concentration on a single word, and then another, and another. This is splendid work, as worthy and demanding as any, and the will and resilience to do it are good for the writer's soul." —Andre Dubus II (1936-1999), from his essay "First Books," in his book *Meditations from a Movable Chair*

2. An orange and black label that reads, "Fragile: handle with care."

3. A bumper sticker advertising "Winter with the Writers," the annual literary festival at Rollins College, my alma mater.

4. A lightweight wooden bookmark from a friend that states, "Though she be but little, she is fierce." From Shakespeare's play *A Midsummer Night's Dream*.

5. "The only story that seems worth writing is a cry, a shot, a scream. A story should break the reader's heart." —Susan Sontag, *As Consciousness Is Harnessed to Flesh: Journals and Notebooks, 1964-1980*.

6. A small red card with two words printed in white letters: "You Matter."

What surrounds you as you sit down to write?

In Magnification

For Wiggles, a Siamese fighting fish we loved

You swirl and twist in liquid dance
blue and red trails floating,
how fast you flutter and quiver
those fins, with every nerve attuned,
you peer, blink-less through the glass.

We study one another
through the clear curved wall,
one of us with bigger brains, the other
full of grace but timid, while all the room
shifts through a water lens
and cool refracted light.

I tap against the vase
a sound like tin cans crashing?
In your hydrodynamic life is that sound
louder than it seems?
You shrink back, motor fiercely away
to bounce into the other side. Believe me,
we are more alike than not.

Unlock Writer's Block

Have you ever wondered whether writer's block is really real, whether it is a true psychological problem that many writers, including myself, often claim thwarts their attempts to write their hearts out on the page without fear? I have.

What Does It Feel Like?
It feels like a wall, some say, that blocks their path on the writing road, prevents them from moving around to the other side where they've traveled before when they wrote. They say, "We *want* to write, but just can't." When that happens, some bear down with fierce determination typified by a scowl, by clenched jaws and knit brows, making the matter worse. I know. I've done all that myself.

Some writers assert writer's block does *not exist*. It's only a term to disguise fear, or laziness, or lack of gumption. It's an excuse, they say, to avoid the work. Just get your butt in the chair, we're told, and do it. Sometimes that's good advice; other times it's not.

If we *want* to write so badly, then why do we avoid it? Like most things, the answer varies per person. It's highly probable that no definitive answer exists to unlock writer's block, but here are a few insights.

What's Really Going with Writer's Block?
The *Beginning Writer's Answer Book*, edited by Kirk Polking, includes

some useful insights on this topic in "Chapter 34: How Do I Cope with Rejections and Writer's Block?"

Q. *What causes writer's block and how can I combat it?*

A. Ask twenty writers what causes writer's block, and you'll probably get twenty different answers. The causes of writer's block usually don't have anything to do with writing, but rather are connected to factors that serve to distract the writer, keeping him from concentrating on his craft. Overwork is one such factor. A writer who is fatigued from overwork should stop writing for a couple of days. Financial worries, personal problems and illnesses all could keep a writer from his work.

Unlock Your Mind, Unblock the Writing

If we're distracted or upset over an unresolved problem, as Polking suggested above, then let's try our best to either solve it or compartmentalize it until we can resolve it. Imagine the problem is a chair. Place it in another room and shut the door. Return to writing. Or write the issue on notepaper and seal it in an envelope to deal with later. Or if it's a matter beyond your control to solve, let it go. Easy for me to say....

Change Your Writing Setup

Sometimes it's the *way* you work that needs to change, not your mind. Perhaps choose another topic to write about. Or instead of composing on a computer, write longhand in a notebook, or on a yellow legal pad. Years ago, my husband, instead of doing the actual writing himself, dictated his book, and another person transcribed it. Maybe what you need is something as simple as a different desk, a new lampshade, or soft music in the background. Experiment.

Remember: you are a writer. Your writing really *does* matter, especially to your own mental (and often physical) health. In Brenda Ueland's gem of a book, *If You Want to Write: A Book about Art, Inde-*

pendence and Spirit, she comforts us: "… Inspiration comes very slowly and quietly." She assures us we "… are going to write, to tell something on paper, sooner or later."

📖 A Book I Recommend about Unlocking Creativity

The Mystery of the Cleaning Lady: A Writer Looks at Creativity and Neuroscience by Australian fiction writer and creative writing professor, Sue Woolfe. Read about her at Goodreads, a website about books and their authors: https://www.goodreads.com/author/show/57117.Sue_Woolfe

Camera-Eyes: A Writing Prompt

Here's a strong cup of hot coffee—a prompt—to get you writing in the morning or any time of day. It's a modified version of an exercise I did in a college class on Human Potentials, a field of psychological study popular in the 1970s. We explored many capacities that we human beings have, including the ability to observe, in a flash, what we see in front of us. As writers, we know that such keen observation is essential.

Eyes as Camera Shutters

One day, our class went outside to a nearby yard, each of us paired up with another student. Around the yard, the pairs of students walked, one person led another (by the hand) who had closed eyes. Each pair decided how long to do this before the students with closed eyes opened them and immediately squeezed them shut again. They used their eyes as a camera to take a photograph of what they saw during that quick look at their environment. After they re-closed their eyes, these "camera" students described to their partner what they remembered from their "flash" of open eyes.

The result was this: we experienced a way of seeing something without gradually considering it in relation to objects around it. By doing this, we minimized our preconceived notions, limited our expectations. When we opened our eyes, *Bam!* there it was, popping out of its context. If I remember correctly, I saw a tree trunk up-close. Viewing it in this sudden way made it more "its own person," so to speak, independent of the ground, sky, other trees. All I saw was gray-brown bark that resembled gigantic lizard skin, right up against my nose.

Close Eyes, Spin—Open Eyes, Write

A few years later, when I began to keep a daily journal, I made up a version of that exercise. I did it while alone in the kitchen before I left for work. I shut my eyes and kept them shut while slowly turning around a couple of times (after I cleared the floor of stuff I might trip over). When I opened my eyes, whatever my gaze fell upon first is what I wrote about for twenty minutes.

Write What You See

I have an antique iron my mother bought when I was a young child. Years later, after she passed away, it was one among a handful of items I kept of hers, and I treasure it. No matter where I live, I make sure it's in plain sight.

When I had an apartment in Tampa, Florida, one morning I did my spin-with-closed-eyes—open-eyes exercise in the kitchen, and guess what I saw first? My mother's antique iron on a nearby shelf. I sat right down in the breakfast nook and wrote about the old iron's color, shape, how the wooden handle detached to be clamped onto another iron waiting on the fire.

As that year went on, I reworked and revised my piece about the iron and shaped it into a poem that eventually won a prize under the title "A Bar Iron," later renamed "A Shirt Not Her Own." It's included below.

If this writing prompt suits your practice, go for it. Watch where you end up spinning. It could be magical.

A Shirt Not Her Own

> *I have an antique iron with a detachable wooden handle enabling users to clamp the handle onto another iron that's been heating on the stove. My mother found the iron in an antique shop when I was a little girl. This poem is for all the women who ever used it.*

By a window a woman,
heavy in her shoes,
labors in the heat,
shoves an iron over a shirt.

The iron steams through wrinkles,
mindless plow through its field.
Steam rises, she barely breathes,
her mind weighted with stone gray years.

She loosens the handle from the iron,
clamps another, ready and hot,
presses another
shirt, not her own.

This woman by the window,
glances up, sees a child at play,
smiles, does not wave.
Her hands hold an iron and a shirt.

Waving, the child spins away.
The woman breathes.
Her hands lay down their chores
and wipe the window clear.

III

WORDS BECOME SENTENCES

Vocabulary, Mysteries, and Prevarication

I admit it: I'm hooked on mysteries. It all started with Nancy Drew. When I was a kid, I'd lie on the couch with my grandmother's quilt pulled up to my chin and immerse myself in those mystery stories, one book after another. Not much has changed over the years. Like every Agatha Christie junkie, I love the challenge of deciphering a whodunit, especially mysteries I watch on television. One of my favorites is *Edderkoppen*, Danish for *Spider*, set in postwar Copenhagen, Sweden. The main character, Bjarne, works as a newspaper reporter who relentlessly investigates a web of greed, corruption, and horrific murders while he falls in love with the "wrong" woman. I'll say no more.

Side-Effect of Subtitles

An aspect I love about international shows (I live in the USA, and English is my native language) is listening to different languages spoken *and* seeing the on-screen English translation. Maybe it's because I not only *hear* the foreign words (which I usually don't understand) but I *see* their translation. The sight of it in bold text across the bottom of the screen makes me pay closer attention to each word than I might have if I'd only *heard* each word spoken aloud by the actors. Maybe. This is just a theory. Or perhaps it's because I totally love words. I'm a writer. You're a writer. We love words; we love sentences. And I suspect that if a character in a show speaks English, some unique words might slip past me in a stream of spoken sentences. However, in a foreign country subtitled situation like *Edderkoppen*, new or provocative words jump out at me.

A *Spider* Word

Because I watched the *Spider* series, one striking word comes to mind when I hear someone hedge in a conversation, hesitate to tell it straight. Near the end of the show, Bjarne and his troubled older brother (who was caught in the crime web Bjarne was investigating) fell into a heated conversation. For some minutes, Bjarne presses his brother for vital information, leans in close to his face. They are in a small room; its confinement intensifies their combative emotions. "Don't prevaricate!" yells Bjarne (of course he said that in Danish, but the subtitle told me the English word). Instantly, his brother relents and spills the truth.

Prevaricate—What We Don't Want to Do

Although I grasped from the context what *prevaricate* meant, I looked it up anyway in Merriam Webster: "to deviate from the truth: equivocate." What a no-no, especially in the context of a crime. Don't stray from the truth or use ambiguous language.

The Power of the Negative Command

Rather than tell his brother what to do (speak the truth), Bjarne tells him what *not* to do. A wonderful part of this scene is that Bjarne is confident his brother's vocabulary is up to the task. No need for him to grab a dictionary. I like this approach of employing a negative command to get a positive response. It wields irresistible power.

What's in Your Vocabulary?

Long ago I had a book about building one's vocabulary. I can't recall the name of it now, but it suggested that you choose an unfamiliar word every day and use it in a sentence as often as possible that same day without annoying everyone around you. By the end of the month, you will have about thirty additional words at your disposal, and, theoretically, you'll be adept at putting them to good use. This month, I'm going to practice with *prevaricate*. How about you?

Building Great Sentences

In the writing game, sentences are baseballs. Although not every sentence brings about a home run, isn't our goal to hit at least one out of the park? To move effective sentences requires aim and power. "The sentence is where we must start if we hope to understand why some writing captivates us and other writing leaves us unmoved." That sound advice is from University of Iowa Professor Dr. Brooks Landon. Just as home runs move fans to stand up and cheer, we want our sentences to move readers to engage their imaginations and feel certain emotions, to bring them to tears, to laughter, to new realizations.

Take Aim

One strategy for capturing the reader's imagination is to compose the kind of sentences categorized as *cumulative*. The Oxford Dictionary defines *cumulative*: "increasing or increased in quantity, degree, or force by successive additions, i.e., 'the cumulative effect of two years of drought.' Synonyms: increasing, accumulative, accumulating, growing, progressive, accruing, snowballing." I think we get the idea. Such a sentence tags each base and slides the reader into home where it counts. Fans aren't captivated by weak fly balls: sentences without a clear destination. What engages readers is crossing home plate: sentences that score.

The Teaching Company, publisher of *The Great Courses: Teaching That Engages the Mind,* produced a two-part course titled *Building Great Sentences: Exploring the Writer's Craft* by Professor Landon. He thoroughly investigates what *cumulative* sentences are, how to build them, and when and how to make them enliven your work.

What are *cumulative* sentences? They grow from a base clause, such as "She re-read chapter one" by piling up modifiers and adding clauses to make it grow into "She re-read chapter one, cleaned the kitchen, and while the kids napped, she finished writing her ten-volume book." Better examples from masterful writers appear below. But first ...

Build Power

Remember in Earth Science class when you learned about cloud formations? In case you missed that day, here's a recap of one formation that sounds like the sort of sentence we're talking about: *cumulus* clouds. Merriam-Webster defines *cumulus*: "1. Heap, accumulation. 2. [New Latin, from Latin]: a dense puffy cloud form having a flat base and rounded outlines often piled up like a mountain." Although we spell the adjective *cumulus* for clouds differently than *cumulative* for sentences, it carries the same idea of piling something onto a base. Next time you notice a *cumulus* cloud, try writing a *cumulative* sentence, as found in these examples. Enjoy!

Examples of Cumulative Sentences

1. Hermann Hesse: "And these men, for whom life has no repose, live at times in their rare moments of happiness with such strength and indescribable beauty, the spray of their moment's happiness is flung so high and dazzlingly over the wide sea of suffering, that the light of it, spreading its radiance, touches others too with its enchantment." From Hesse's book *Steppenwolf*.

2. Albert Camus: "But in those days when the plague seemed to be retreating, slinking back to the obscure lair from which it had stealthily emerged, at least one person in the town viewed this retreat with consternation, if Tarrou's

notes are to be trusted: and that man was Cottard." From Camus' book *The Plague*.

3. Annie Dillard: "Yes, you say, as if you'd been asleep a hundred years, this is it, this is the real weather, the lavender light fading, the full moisture in your lungs, the heat from the pavement on your lips and palms—not the dry orange dust from horses' hooves, the salt sea, the sour Coke—but this solid air, the blood pumping up your thighs again, your fingers alive." From Dillard's book *Pilgrim at Tinker Creek*.

📖 Books I Recommend about Sentences

Getting the Words Right, Second Edition: 39 Ways to Improve Your Writing by Theodore A. Rees Cheney

How to Write a Sentence: And How to Read One by Stanley Fish

A Dash of Style: The Art and Mastery of Punctuation by Noah Lukeman

Word Jumble Game

Looking to add some fun to your writing life? You may enjoy this playful exercise: combine words that don't really go together, such as "happy tables." Then make sense of them somehow as you begin a story or start a poem. This exercise is a type of puzzle based on a fun task I experienced years ago in a poetry workshop conducted by poet Dionisio Martinez in Tampa, Florida, as part of a program called *The Writer's Voice*. Martinez helped us tap into our imaginations' storehouse of images, experiment with unusual ideas, and play with words during our wordsmith arts and crafts time. Here's the exercise:

1. Take a page of lined notebook paper and number the first ten lines down the page.
2. Divide the page lengthwise into three columns by drawing lines to divide them.
3. In the first column, write a list of ten nouns, one noun per line, jotting down whatever pops into your mind, e.g., dog, eggs, book, etc.
4. In the second column, do the same with ten random adjectives, e.g., lavender, warm, deranged, etc.
5. In the third column, list ten verbs, e.g., memorizes, screams, steals, etc.

Result: You have three columns on a sheet of lined paper, each column containing ten words. If you want, cut the columns apart and experiment with different match-ups later.

Pick and Choose

Now's the fun part, what I call gluing phrases together. Read aloud the words on the top lines of each column. My example words yielded this nonsensical sentence: *Lavender dog memorizes*. Of course, we've heard about those dogs, right?

Make Sense of Nonsense

Now what? Options are endless. Throw out that *lavender dog* silliness or try to work with it. Let's work with it and see what happens. I began a fairytale.

> Once upon a time, a little princess had a stuffed animal, a silk lavender dog with dark button eyes that, whenever she held him close, looked as though he were memorizing her face.

Or trash that and read the next line down. In my example, you'd get: *Warm eggs scream*. Make a sentence with it: "*Warm eggs scream, 'Gobble me up!'*" Have some fun with that. Or not. Continue on down the list. Or, to make new three-word starters, draw a line from a random adjective in the first column to a noun farther down the page, then back up to a verb near the top of its column. Or make entirely new lists of words. Keep some of them. Toss some out. Jumble the lists around, swap out words to come up with whatever phrases you like. Try them out in fiction, poetry, or a travel story. The point is to fire up your inventiveness, enjoy the sound of language, and create scraps of writing that most likely have never existed.

Dr. Metaphor and Tadpole

Figures of speech can entertain readers and enliven our poems and stories. My favorite is *metaphor*. There's an old silly saying, "What's a metaphor?" I say metaphors perform enhancing jobs, like surgeons. As a surgeon, a metaphor can inject life into a tired sentence, replace a worn-out cliché, and heal a broken story. Merriam-Webster tells us metaphor is "a figure of speech in which a word or phrase literally denoting one kind of object or idea is used in place of another to suggest a likeness or analogy between them (as in *drowning in money*)." Or as in "metaphors are surgeons." (If I'd used *simile* instead of *metaphor*, we'd have *metaphors are like surgeons*.)

Metaphor—What's It to You?
Metaphors are everywhere. Even *you* might be a metaphor. Think about your childhood. Here's a vignette from mine. During the summer when I was eight years old, my mother arranged for me to take swimming lessons at the only house in our neighborhood with a built-in swimming pool. My teacher, Sylvia (not her real name), was a big sister in a bathing suit. As her only student, I received a unique gift: 100 percent of her attention focused on me: a squirmy, splashy, wannabe swimmer. Two mornings a week, in my bright red tank suit, I climbed down the curved concrete steps in the pool's corner and shivered into the water. At Sylvia's, I learned and practiced the American crawl, the backstroke, the side stroke. Out of the corner of my eye, the

diving board summoned, and I hoped that by the end of summer I'd be brave enough to jump off it.

One day I struggled to do the side stroke, while Sylvia cheered me on from her usual position on the pool deck, her silver whistle dangling from a chain around her neck. Suddenly I heard her call out, "Keep it up, Tadpole!" *Tadpole?*

Good old Merriam-Webster tells us a tadpole is a "Frog or toad larva that has a rounded body with a long tail bordered by fins and external gills soon replaced by internal gills and that undergoes a metamorphosis to the adult." Sylvia saw me as a little larva, eventually outgrowing my little red swimsuit and diving like a frog off the board. In becoming a swimmer, I had also become a metaphor.

Use Appropriate Metaphors

In *Self-Editing for Fiction Writers* by Renni Browne and Dave King (I think this is one of the best on the topic), the authors point out that metaphors should be appropriate to their context and not draw attention to themselves. I can't emphasize enough this caution about how to use them. Here's an example from the book showing what NOT to do. It's from a draft of Peter Cooper's novel *Billy Shakes*:

> "As a matter of fact, Lucy, it may be that Rose is pregnant." His eyes were a dark, dark blue, stolen jewels in a setting of bone. "But I can assure you that I am not the father."

Browne and King point out:

> The metaphor, **the dark blue stolen jewels in a setting of bone,** [my bold] strains for effect. Yet the problem isn't the unworkability of the metaphor but its presence in the scene in the first place.

I agree. It's a dark blue ring in a bowl of chicken soup.

Other Minds on Metaphor

Years ago, while I prowled around a used bookstore, I found an enjoyable and thought-provoking book about linguistics and philosophy by George Lakoff and Mark Johnson titled *Metaphors We Live By*. The authors make a strong case showing how metaphors are built into the way we think.

> The essence of metaphor is understanding and experiencing one kind of thing in terms of another.... [H]uman thought processes are largely metaphorical. This is what we mean when we say that the human conceptual system is metaphorically structured and defined. Metaphors as linguistic expressions are possible precisely because there are metaphors in a person's conceptual system.

The authors provide abundant examples, including ones about how we view time as money: "I don't have the time to give you." "How do you spend your time these days?" and how we conceive of argument as war: "Your claims are indefensible." "I demolished his argument."

Off the Diving Board

Now, back to Tadpole. While you work on your next poem, play, story, novel, memoir, historical narrative, science fiction novel, children's book, or self-help book, take time to brainstorm metaphors that may fit well with your theme. Maybe one you've never heard or used before; and avoid clichés like, "Her friend is a couch potato." Perhaps give your piece a metaphorical title. For my memoir, I chose *Undertow*, a metaphor tied to specific events disclosed in the story. *Undertow* was my high-dive off the board. What's yours?

He Was the Grounded Grass

He plumbed the earth until roots wound their way inside.
He was the rich darkness where they found a way to grow.
He was the grounded grass.
He inched along the cracks.

He was the lake where time dove to the bottom.
He sprang up where lions form listening stones.
He kicked the dry stalks away.
He was the threshold of green.

Past   Now   Future

*"You think about the past too much.
Move on."*

What else can we remember?
The past, as stone, has pressed us—
we are insects amber-framed.
Here is our everlasting view.

*"You worry over the future too much.
Live Now."*

But Now mothers our next sigh,
trembles her open palm where we lie
in a puff of breath between
then and next, creating the next …

Now, nurse most solemn, stitches
past to future.
There—in the thread,
hidden—in the silk of it—
I wait.

Diction: Desire Pickiness

Diction is being picky about words. "Picky, picky, picky," my mother lamented whenever I whined about my food at mealtime. I wanted *borders* on my plate. I cringed at green beans rolling into mashed potatoes or meatloaf touching corn. "It all goes to the same place," she'd say. Still, I persisted in moving food apart. Why? Taste matters. Our writing all goes to the same place, too: a reader's mind. But we don't heap word upon word willy-nilly like inappropriately spooning globs of peanut butter to crown a heap of spaghetti—yuck! We make vibrant distinctions, consider innuendos, seek the best possible vocabulary, the most appropriate nouns, adjectives and verbs to convey our intentions. (We should try not to use too many adverbs. That advice is from more than a few writers and teachers of writing.) This striving for the best word is integral to what we do. We *must* be picky. That's not a criticism; it's a compliment.

Three Jobs of *Diction*

Merriam-Webster tells us *diction* is the "choice of words especially with regard to correctness, clearness, or effectiveness." That's a three-part job. We dig into diction to search for the *correct*, the *clearest,* and most *effective* word to make our writing shine. Doing this takes time and reflection, research and study, but to produce work well done, the extra effort is worthwhile. When we need some help along the way, where can we go? To where diction lives, of course.

Peruse the Diction-ary

I felt a little silly when I looked up the word *dictionary* in a dictionary ... but who cares? Merriam-Webster tells us *dictionary* is "a reference source in print or electronic form containing words usually alphabetically arranged along with information about their forms, pronunciations, functions, etymologies, meanings, and syntactic and idiomatic uses." By the way, when I discover a word's etymology, I get to know its personal story, and that makes me love it more.

Dictionaries are gold mines where we dig for words, and so are dictionaries' cousins, thesauruses. Both are a writer's treasure trove of options. If you're lucky to have access to the *Oxford English Dictionary* (OED)—you must pay to subscribe or use a library that does—you'll find some super-duper word stories about the first use of any, and I mean *any*, given word in the English language. That search can reveal more ideas and other interesting words you might use. For a fun break from rewriting (all writing is rewriting), check out the OED website. Or any dictionary. Spend an hour dedicated to diction-gone-wild. Or check out *The Professor and the Madman: A Tale of Murder, Insanity, and the Making of the Oxford English Dictionary* by Simon Winchester. It's an utterly remarkable story of the people who made that paragon of lexical aides and how they did it.[2]

Diction in Action

Liven up your diction with words connoting motion. Here's a memorable sentence from Anne Lamott's wonderful book *Bird by Bird: Some Instructions on Writing and Life.*

> I don't mind if a person has no hope if he or she is sufficiently funny about the whole thing, but then, this being able to be funny definitely speaks of a kind of hope, of buoyancy.

Notice one of her picky words: *buoyancy*. When I hear that word, I

---

[2] You might also like the movie version by the same title, *The Professor and the Madman*, starring Sean Penn, Mel Gibson, and Eddie Marsan.

think of a jack-in-the-box toy—when you open the box's lid, a clown on a metal spring pops up and bobs around for a moment, as if afloat on the water's surface. Lamott uses buoyancy again on the very last page of the book when she writes of her students:

"So why does our writing matter, again?" they ask.

> Because of the spirit, I say. Because of the heart. Writing and reading decrease our sense of isolation. They deepen and widen and expand our sense of life: they feed the soul. When writers make us shake our heads with the exactness of their prose and their truths, and even make us laugh about ourselves or life, our buoyancy is restored.

Buoyancy even *sounds* like what it means. Merriam-Webster:

- 1a: the tendency of a body to float or to rise when submerged in a fluid testing an object's buoyancy.
- 1b: chemistry: the power of a fluid to exert an upward force on a body placed in it. also: the upward force exerted.
- 2: the ability to recover quickly from depression or discouragement: RESILIENCE.

Think of someone pushing a beach ball under water in a swimming pool, but the beach ball will not stay down. It pops up again and again. Like hope. Hope doesn't allow a person to stay down. What if Anne Lamott had chosen that synonym, *resilience*? Wouldn't the sound affect you differently? Doesn't it convey an image or sensation other than *buoyancy*? I think Lamott chose the prefect word here, one that evokes resilience but connects us to emotions and ideas that support the idea of funniness and hope: lightness, bubbles, movement, such as a child at Grandma's house who bounces on her big bed, happy and free.

Diction is subjective and depends on a writer's taste. In my view, Lamott's picky word *buoyancy* is perfect for those two sentences. It is clear, correct, and effective. Let's all be picky, picky, picky like that.

P.S. Don't Forget the Thesaurus

Like a clean eraser, keep a thesaurus handy. It helps you find substitutes for shopworn words. It's easy to use an online version. For instance, in your story's Word document, double-click on a word, right-click, select Synonyms, and at the bottom of the list, click Thesaurus. Or keep a paperback version on your desk. I like Roget's. The recent version contains more than 400,000 words. Just be sure to get a good one, not a lousy one.

"I own the world's worst thesaurus. Not only is it awful, it's awful."
—Anonymous

Dust

Not the kind you wipe away
with dust mitts or feathers

Not the kind that rolls into balls under the bed
or floats in rays of sun and cats chase after.

But the kind that imperceptibly accumulates,
out of the corner of your eye as it gains on you
a little worry here
a little doubt there
a little too many T-shirts in the drawer.

One day the dust mitt works no longer, so
you run rather than walk, run
with the panic of lizards, run
with the fear of rabbits into the hedge, run
and run and run past the black anhinga drying its wings,
startled off the log, lifting into the breeze,
and you envy its untethered flight, its
smooth arc above the lake into
a broad, unfettered sky.

Tighten Up: Cut the Clichés

Remember the song "Tighten Up" by the R&B group Archie Bell & the Drells, a 1968 #1 hit? Those of us of a certain age do. One day I woke up humming that song and a connection to the writing process occurred to me. What connection? A major writing habit that some refer to as an illness: lazy writing. We need to heal ourselves of that. One way is to change our writing diet. Let's start with eliminating clichés. But first, what is a cliché, anyway?

Merriam-Webster: Clichés 101

Definition of *cliché:*
1: a trite phrase or expression, also: the idea expressed by it
2: a hackneyed theme, characterization, or situation
3: something (such as a menu item) that has become overly familiar or commonplace

Cut Clichés

Really? Cut all of them out? Aren't clichés useful tools to connect us with readers, to wiggle our way into their minds with a set-in-place, popular vocabulary? Meet them in familiar territory? As if in the open square of our book's small town? Perhaps. But to create more original work, I suggest we try and banish clichés—those overused and overworked words or phrases we've heard so many times they seem hardwired into our vocabulary. Examples: "Dry as a bone," "In the heat of the moment," and "Old as the hills." Also, one-word clichés exist, at least in my opinion, such as "amazing," probably the most over-used word jumping about like popcorn in blogs, social media, magazines, and newspapers. There's: "Sit in our courtyard or our verandah, both of which are amazing," and "The pineapple pizza was just amazing," and "Wasn't the concert totally amazing?" and "Her amazing haircut made her look years younger. Just amazing!"

I say pour some de-greaser down our cliché-clogged writerly brain-drains, clean out those boring phrases, and open our creative flow. Put some thought into finding synonyms or unusual but poignant comparisons, find new ways of saying the same old things. Oops. I just realized I used "the same old things" and now that's in the grip of what I call the cliché-catcher; it deserves some loving tighten-up treatment. Just like "a long story short." What are your downfalls, your junk food phrases, your clichés?

Cliché-Catcher

I already mentioned "old as the hills." Another that shows up at the new year and on birthdays is "Time flies." Where's that cliché-catcher? We are lucky when we find friends to read our work and act as our personal cliché-catchers. That's one value of writers' groups or long-distance writer pals. Even book clubs.

One month, my book club read *Only to Sleep,* a novel by Lawrence Osborne that brought his character, Raymond Chandler Phillip Marlowe, back to life as an aging detective. Osborne, to his credit, has not used "old as the hills" in his book, but he does describe Marlowe as "old man" repeatedly. That description really got on my nerves.

Alternative to "Old Man"

I am aware I should avoid "older than dirt," but what is an original substitute? Maybe we don't need an alternative phrase, just an alternative approach. One way of showing a character's advanced age (and avoid agism) might be to have them do something that *shows* they, like

Marlowe, are past eighty (an arbitrary number for illustrative purposes only; please don't take it personally.) Our hero Marlowe is often in hotel bars. Rather than having him lean on the bar to drink his gin and tonic, to his credit, Osborne has Marlowe sit at a table because it's easier than climbing up on a barstool. And he adds something else…

Do the Tighten Up

To show how Marlowe copes with physical limitations, Osborne gives Marlowe a cane. It's ingenious, really, because the cane not only helps Marlowe keep his balance, hike rocky inclines, and push open doors, it also adds another dimension to the story. Spoiler alert: hidden in the cane's handle is a knife—a feature that helps low-key Marlowe compensate for his shaky legs and gain an advantage over off-guard adversaries.

Try to clean up your stories by identifying and cutting out overused phrases and ideas that sneak into your work. Take a moment and listen to Archie and his friends belt out their catchy song.[3] I hope it helps you remember to "Do the Tighten Up" and think, "Cut clichés!"

---

[3] https://www.youtube.com/watch?v=Wro3bqi4Eb8.

Nothing Like a Smooth Transition

In Stephen King's no-nonsense guide *On Writing: A Memoir of the Craft*, he includes a chapter titled "What Writing Is." Drum roll. Finally, we're going to find out the nature of this mysterious activity. What does King tell us it is? "Telepathy, of course."

He elucidates: when we write, we're simply sending, by way of words, our thoughts into readers' minds. That's our aim—to transfer in a provocative, entertaining, informative, well-structured, and compelling way, what is alive in our minds without confusing our readers.

Clear Telepathy

We want no static to interfere with our message. How do we accomplish such a telepathic effect? We employ strong writing skills. One of the most crucial skills to develop is crafting effective transitions. It takes thoughtful practice. One of our responsibilities as writers is to create unmuddied, sensible ways of moving readers through our writing until they reach the end—and ask for more.

Trains of Transitions

Writers say, "Here, read, and follow my train of thought." A coherent story is a train of thought with efficient transitions. When your story is cogent, it runs unimpeded along its tracks, carrying readers in their comfy padded seats from one location to the next. You transfer them to various places: one character to a different character, one time-period to another, one idea or emotion to a new one. Transitions can happen within one sentence, from one sentence to the next, from one paragraph to the next, from one chapter to the next. If you write transitions in a rough or unclear fashion, it's as if your train has hit a downed tree strewn across the tracks, or even worse, your story-train has jumped the tracks and lost your readers. What to do?

A Suggestion for a Smooth Transition
For instance, try this: in the first sentence of a new scene, tell the reader how much time has gone by. Here's an excerpt that demonstrates this from James Sullivan's heart-wrenching memoir about the difficulties and joys of falling in love with a Vietnamese woman in her home country: *Over the Moat: Love Among the Ruins of Imperial Vietnam*:

> If they want to keep you out, she told me, they can. I countered her story with Gary. Gary always found a way back in, and if he could, why couldn't I?
>
> I went to sleep on that little bit of solace and in the morning buoyed up out of sleep into sunshine.

* * *

Fun fact: In 2009, I traveled to Vietnam with my husband, Hoyt. Just before arriving, I finished reading Sullivan's memoir, which I'd found in a bookstore in Ubud, Bali, Indonesia, where we lived for two months prior to visiting Vietnam. Looking back on that time, I see how reading Sullivan's story pre-sensitized me to the areas we visited. For instance, when we were in Hue, the old imperial city where Sullivan met the woman he fell in love with, I felt very close to the place; an ease entered my soul. I *had* been there before: I'd seen it, smelled it, and sensed all of it in my imagination while reading that memoir. And that book helped me appreciate more my own experience among the Vietnamese people, the history of their country, the beauty of that verdant land. Before you do any traveling, I recommend reading memoirs that take place in your destination. You may feel a unique kinship with the people and the place.

* * *

Clear and Present Transitions

In learning any craft, the wise apprentice studies the masters. In writing, the masters are authors who've proven their skills, who've carried many readers along their story-tracks in smooth reading bliss. One such master is the author and teacher Theodore A. Rees Cheney, who included a chapter about transitions in his book *Getting the Words Right, Second Edition: 39 Ways to Improve Your Writing*.

> A writer's goal is to move from sentence to sentence and paragraph to paragraph without jarring the reader—unless it is his intention to do so. The writer should be considerate enough to lead the reader across a bridge—not force the poor soul to leap across a chasm in the dark. Some writers fool themselves, assuming that such leaps are easy for any reader of intelligence. It is relatively easy to leap to the next thought without a bridge, provided you know how much of a running start to take, how high to leap, and where you're going to land. The writer knows all this in advance; the reader does not.

Read Aloud to Improve Transitions

A powerful method to identify weak or absent transitions (to remove any trees lying across the tracks) is to read your work aloud. Stand in front of a mirror or sit alone in a room and read your sentences, one after another, out loud—do not mumble—so that someone in the next room could hear them. When you listen to yourself saying sentences aloud, pronouncing each word precisely, you more easily catch missing words, cumbersome phrases, and illogical or rough transitions.

Mark each place where you stumbled as you read aloud. Next, study the context to figure out how to smooth the ride. As you concentrate on making each transition more effective, remember your goal is to keep readers on track, following your train of thought, reading your mind, receiving your message. When they read THE END, they'll be glad they heeded your call to, "Hop aboard this story-train. It will deliver."

IV
WRITING MEMOIR

Christine

A chaser after fireflies I was,
while Christine hobbled by
Mom's irises and lilies.
Summer nearly gone,
grassy scents filled our hair, bathed our skin.

I grabbed at blinking bugs, soft bodies
slow like drugged evasive dreams.

Hedges and thorns silhouetted
in evening's lilac light,
twinkled and flashed with yellow, bright.

Christine leaned and laughed
at my attempts to trap those flying beetles,
her voice a cheer for them or me
I couldn't tell.

My nimble body running,
her crutch thumped heavy, dull,
her one leg skipped ahead.

I never told her: *In heaven we'll be perfect,
you'll get a new leg then
like Sister Mary Margaret said.*
Never asked, *"Don't you wish you had it now?"*

How she lost it,
how it felt to take a bath
with one leg missing, one leg there,
I never could quite ask her. No, no, never could.

Memoir: Whose Story Is It Anyway?

If you're an author, do you give book talks? I know, they are full of wildcards and unexpected questions. A bit unnerving. Most people who showed up for my book events for *Undertow* were friendly and interested—except for that one woman who accused me of not believing in anything and stomped out of the room. We had good reason to suspect she'd had too much to drink. Oh well. Stuff happens.

So, about giving talks regarding my memoir *Undertow*. I'm retired from doing that now, but here are some things I experienced. Depending on the audience, I focused on different aspects of the story. At some presentations, I discussed cults more than fundamentalism. At others, the reverse was true. For presentations mainly for writers, I talked about my experiences writing the book. I shared the importance of finding a knowledgeable editor(s) and some lessons learned; e.g., it's worth your while to study how to construct lively and effective dialogue. It's not as easy as you might think. Here again is where reading aloud can help catch mistakes of all sorts and correct bumpy sentences.

Helpful hint: Read aloud *short* sections of text at a time. Take breaks. Don't do what I did. One day I read aloud so much of *Undertow* (a longer book than this one) that before I realized it, I had a sore throat; I had to run to the store to buy lemon lozenges. I'm not used to doing a whole lot of talking in one sitting.

At some writerly events, I offered a handout with the timeline showing *Undertow*'s journey from conception to birth—no light matter. (Find it in Appendix 1 of this book.) For those interested, I also offered a list of books that help me be a better writer. Notice I say "help" not "helped." I'm still learning. I include the list at the end of this essay.

Back to memoirs. Something important I've found out is that many people haven't read many memoirs, if any at all, and they ask how in the world did I remember all those details in my book? To answer, one thing I tell them is that to construct the story I used not only my memories but source materials I kept over the years. The other thing I say is, "Let's talk about what memoir *is*."

What is Memoir?
Memoirs are true stories written in the first person about a portion of the author's life, along with the author's current-day reflections on that part of their life—hopefully after a good amount of time has passed. It's that long-view perspective in memoir that gives it richness, depth, and meaning.

Flashing light: The point of writing a memoir is not only to share experiences, but catapult them to a level of general interest and insight. Memoirs read more like fiction (a novel) or creative nonfiction rather than autobiography, which relates a life's events one after another.

As writers, we need to remember that our story, including the events we share, the feelings we express, and our in-the-rearview-mirror reflections, is *ours*. Other people are in it, but we must focus on telling our personal tale. That was one of my biggest challenges with the story in *Undertow*. A lot of other people besides me are in it, and they maintain many different perspectives on "What happened during the heydays of The Way International."

Memoirists aim to capture what's called "emotional truth" in each scene of the book to convey their story's heart to the reader. On this topic of writing memoir, you can find lots of books, take many classes, and even get a specialized PhD. It's vast. While I was a student at Rollins College, I took two in-depth classes about autobiography/memoir. I've read stacks and stacks of other people's memoirs. They are all different, but in so many ways they are all the same.

Memoir: It's All about You and It's NOT All about You

"It's all about you" sounds pretty egotistical. But memoirs don't have to be an ego trip via words. They are a brief trip through the writer's life showing some sort of lesson or insight. It's the lesson learned that makes the story "NOT all about you." Readers want to know what you learned, how you grew or changed, what is the upshot of the experience for you.

I think an important question to ask about a memoir is why the writer engaged in the project; what is the writer's intention in telling this particular slice of their story? In my view, revenge is not good or appropriate in memoir. (Revenge, if it's worthwhile anywhere, is better perpetrated in fiction with identities changed or hidden.) Remember that old saying, "Living well is the best revenge." Instead of getting even, let's get busy sharing our understanding of the human condition. Let's aim to enlighten. Or to warn. Or to heal or comfort. Or to educate or entertain, or to weave these intentions together in a tapestry, as best we can.

Upfront—Front Matter That Matters

I believe writers have a responsibility to make clear the genre of their book. With your memoir, be sure readers know that they are reading a true story, a section from your actual life. When readers open any book, they need to know what genre the content falls into. This creates understanding between them and the author, like a reading contract. They want to know: is this fiction? Historical fiction? Nonfiction? Memoir is categorized as nonfiction. Usually, you see this point made on a book's cover or in the preface or introduction.

The following are some points I made in the front matter of my memoir (mostly in the preface) to let readers know the nature of *Undertow*. I hope you find this list useful.

1. This book is a work of nonfiction; it is a memoir.
2. It is my recollection of events related to the best of my knowledge and ability.
3. The story's crucial facts are true.
4. Some events and conversations are combined in the interest of storytelling.
5. Besides my memory and bits from others' memories, my sources include my extensive collection of notes, journals, letters, calendars, books, newspapers, photographs, and copies of *The Way Magazine*.
6. I have not changed any names except the ones listed here. (Refer to *Undertow's* Preface for these details.)
7. For privacy reasons, other identities have been altered or made composites.
8. I recognize others' memories or interpretations of the events I describe herein may be different from my own. (This point is CRUCIAL to make, in my opinion.)

By the way, my daughter, who is now an adult, tells me I have a kick-a** memory, so there's that. Some things you just never forget! And some conversations in the book are from notes I wrote immediately after the conversations. I think I was born with a documentation gene. So, there's that, too.

And one more thing: several readers, including former followers of The Way International (the cult I spent seventeen years in), read drafts and fact-checked things for me—every writer needs to get their verifiable facts straight. Those folks are my heroes, and I credit them in the Acknowledgments of *Undertow*.

Bit of Advice

If you're going to publish your memoir, hire a copy editor / line editor to scour the final draft. This is a specialized skill. Not all editors do it. Ask around for recommendations.[4]

📖 Books I Recommend That Help Me Be a Better Writer

The Art of Subtext by Charles Baxter

Self-Editing for Fiction Writers by Renni Browne & Dave King

The Artist's Way: A Spiritual Path to Higher Creativity by Julia Cameron

Getting the Words Right, Second Edition: 39 Ways to Improve Your Writing by Theodore A. Rees Cheney

The Writing Life by Annie Dillard

Writing with Power: Techniques for Mastering the Writing Process by Peter Elbow

How to Write a Sentence: And How to Read One by Stanley Fish

The Situation and the Story by Vivian Gornick

The Triggering Town: Lectures and Essays on Poetry and Writing by Richard Hugo

The First Five Pages by Noah Lukeman

MFA in a Box: A Why to Write Book by John Rember

The Philosophy of Rhetoric by I. A. Richards

The Scene Book: A Primer for the Fiction Writer by Sandra Scofield

If You Want to Write: A Book about Art, Independence and Spirit by Brenda Ueland

On Writing Well: An Informal Guide to Writing Nonfiction by William Zinsser

---

[4] For advice on when to hire an editor, here's a good source: https://www.writersdigest.com/publishing-faqs/when-to-hire-an-editor-expert-opinions.

📖 Books I Recommend Specifically on Writing Memoir

Writing the Memoir: From Truth to Art by Judith Barrington

Composing a Life by Mary Catherine Bateson

The Business of Memoir: The Art of Remembering in an Age of Forgetting by Charles Baxter

The Art of Time in Memoir: Then, Again by Sven Birkerts

The Art of Memoir by Mary Karr

I Could Tell You Stories: Sojourns in the Land of Memory by Patricia Hampl

Your Life as Story: Discovering the "New Autobiography" and Writing Memoir as Literature by Tristine Rainer

False Moves

For my mother, Anne R. Lamy
June 8, 1920–November 27, 1968

Just past midnight, I turned the kitchen doorknob,
but the click and slide of the latch signaled our escape.
My friend and I held still as twins, breathing.

Upstairs, Mother being Mother heard the click and
in seconds she was on the stairs,
her shriek pierced the night—
"Girls! What are you doing?"

"Uh, nothing," I called and huddled by the door,
peeking through its windowpane,
begging heaven's help to venture down.
Instead, pine trees blocked our rescue.

"Come here!" Mother cried.
We stood chastened in the living room
as she griped the banister midway to us,
green curlers askew on her head,
her terry robe wound tight, her face awash with fear.
"And just where did you think you were going?"

"Nowhere, really. Just out." I shrank with the lie.
"Out?" she nodded and buttoned up her anger.
"You could get … hurt … out … there."

My girlfriend's father arrived, shaken from the call.
In shame, I watched him march his daughter out.

I imagine the woman on the stairs was shattered.
I imagine, when she lay dying soon thereafter,
beyond the reach of anyone,
had my last move in her direction not
been slowed by dumb rebellion,
I might now be spared what I remember:
she was gone without a word,
left without a final word from me.

Differences Between Memoir and Autobiography

Are you writing a memoir? An autobiography? Do you know the difference between the two forms? In 2009, while my husband and I were on an overseas trip, I received a lesson in an outdoor classroom about the difference between autobiography and memoir. My teacher? A small brown snail.

The snail lived in Indonesia, on the island of Bali, where I met him when we stayed for two months in a traditional Balinese hotel in the town of Ubud. My husband was doing research in Bali, poor guy, but someone has to do it, right? One feature of the hotel was an outdoor dining area, its architecture pavilion-like, which is common in Bali. The entire hotel compound was set in a jungle garden of tropical plants and orange, pink, and white flowers. We had breakfast every morning shaded and cooled in the pavilion.

One morning, in the foliage near our breakfast table, a little snail appeared. It crept fairly close to me, its conical house riding on its back. When I noticed it, I dropped my fork, grabbed my camera, and took a series of photos of that little guy to chronicle its travels over, under, around, and up the broad, bright green leaves. I had plenty of time to click, click, click while that snail skulked along, since (yeah, I know) it moved at a snail's pace.

Memoir or Autobiography?

That warm and sunny morning, my photographs of the little creature's journey captured only a few adventurous moments of its life. Afterward, as I reflected on that session, I thought it was a good example for showing the difference between memoir and autobiography. At the time, I was writing a memoir (*Undertow*), and several friends had asked about the difference.

Memoir

The word "memoir" comes from the Latin word *memoria*, translated "memory."[5] Like my snail friend's leafy adventure, memoir is a slice of someone's life told in a story that can read like a novel, or take other forms, such as a series of related essays. For more on memoir forms, refer to Julia Barrington's book *Writing the Memoir: From Truth to Art*.

An author of memoir writes about a segment of their personal *true* story, but what makes a memoir a memoir? It includes reflections on the author's life from their current point of view. That is the main hallmark of the genre. For example, if my Balinese snail friend wrote a memoir, it might go like this:

> One day alongside the breakfast pavilion at what I call Hotel Paradise, I was inching my way along a large green leaf, when suddenly, this eccentric tourist lady spent about half an hour taking pictures of me. I was desperately shy. My parents (also shy) certainly had never prepared me for paparazzi. Considering my picture is now all over the Internet, I appreciate the attention. Usually I am ignored, since all I do is just crawl around in the background, but by capturing me in photos, this lady has made me believe I am important and beautiful.

By nature, memoirs are subjective, not as objective as investigative journalism should be or official biographies or autobiographies; however, memoir writers should do their best to research whatever facts they write about things, people, and places. One of my favorite memoirs is Michael Ondaatje's *Running in the Family*. I love the way he

---

5   https://www.merriam-webster.com/dictionary/memory#learn-more.

describes the oddball characters in his family, the hilarious situations they fall into, and the haunting, intense, and unpredictable jungle atmosphere of Sri Lanka—where he was born and raised. Ondaatje's writing is poetic and simply beautiful. On the back cover of the paperback edition I have, we see this endorsement from brilliant Margaret Atwood, "… Brightly colored, sweet and painful, bloody-minded and other-worldly, [this book] achieves the status of legend."

So, there's a *then* and a *now* aspect in a memoir that, if you're not used to reading or writing one, may seem odd at first. If what you are used to reading is fiction or journalism or other forms of writing that do not interweave *then* and *now* perspectives, then memoir will give you a new genre to explore.

Autobiography

Merriam-Webster tells us an autobiography is "a biography written by the person it is about." Unlike memoir, which is only a slice of life, autobiography is *nearly* the whole pie (I know what you're thinking … it cannot go to the very end.) It's *auto* (self) *bio* (life) *graphy* (writing).

Autobiography involves some reflection as well, otherwise it is pretty dry, but reflection tends not to be as big a feature as it is in memoir, because the emphasis in memoir is on remembering *and* reflecting on what is remembered, not *chronicling* a life, i.e. I was born, then this happened, and that happened, etc. Some autobiographies are more artfully written than that, but you get the idea. Here's one of interest: *Me: Elton John Official Autobiography*.

Why I Had to Escape a Fundamentalist Cult

Note: This is a slightly edited version of the essay first published in ICSA Today *prior to the publication of my memoir,* Undertow. *Reprinted with permission of the International Cultic Studies Association.*

I was a born-again college freshman in 1970 when sincere Christians recruited me into The Way International, founded by Victor Paul Wierwille. He marketed his organization as a biblical research, teaching, and fellowship ministry, but it was a fundamentalist cult that grew to about 40,000 graduates of Wierwille's classes worldwide. I had only wanted to know, love, and serve God and understand the Bible—what harm could that possibly bring? After seventeen years in the cult, I realized some of the harm it had brought me.

The harm originated with Wierwille's character—he was a charismatic, authoritarian fundamentalist, a dangerous mix—and his non-negotiable belief in the inerrancy of Scripture, which he used fear to compel others to share. While I worked at Way headquarters from 1984 to 1987, the final years of my involvement, I awakened to the reality that Wierwille did not teach "the accurate Word of God" as he'd claimed, nor was he the man of God I had believed in. For my own well-being, I had to escape.

How I Got in The Way

In college I was searching for more than a degree in English. I wanted truth. At the time, college campuses around the United States were coping with student demonstrations raging against the Vietnam War. A protest at Kent State University in Ohio, a few months before I entered college, ended in tragedy. The National Guard opened fire. They killed four students and seriously injured nine. Outrage, confusion, and fear ensued.

Concurrently, an active Jesus movement in pockets around the nation attracted young people seeking answers in a world gone mad. "Jesus freaks" spread a message of love and peace and Bible reading. The Way followers I met on the East Carolina University campus were different. They said their group was a serious, organized, nondenominational ministry doing significant biblical research. It was a nonprofit organization; that appealed to me. So did the members' friendliness and certainty about God's Word having all the answers for life.

About the Way International
Victor Paul Wierwille (1916–1985) started The Way in 1942. During the late 1960s, the organization was tearing across America, thanks to hippies recruited in San Francisco, Kansas, and New York, and college students in North Carolina systematically spreading its message. The basic outreach tool used to promote The Way was Wierwille's two-week Bible class, "The Foundational Class on Power for Abundant Living." Wierwille taught what he called special keys to unlock the true interpretation of the Bible, "the accuracy of the Word." He quoted Scripture verses to support everything he said. He acted and sounded convincing.

My Initial Trauma
What made me vulnerable to The Way? I was raised in the Roman Catholic faith. In 1968 when I was sixteen, my mother died of cancer. Devastation overtook me, and I fell into a pit of grief. Infuriated by my father's Catholic platitudes of "God took your mother," I began to ask questions. "What kind of God takes away mothers?" I needed her more on earth than God needed her in heaven. My father grew dis-

tant, struggling to process his own grief. With my older sister married and living far away and no other relatives around, I felt lost, alone, and abandoned.

Growing up Catholic, I had taken for granted that the authority on how to live for God and what to believe as true was partly the Scriptures, but *really* the Pope and 2,000 years of tradition that formed our esoteric rituals at Mass, and righteous attitudes, such as believing Protestants were damned. Since the Scriptures only augmented the Church fathers' authority, I knew only a little of it. Instead of the Bible, in Catholic school I internalized questions and answers carved in the stone tablet of the Baltimore Catechism, the standard tool for converting young minds to the doctrines of the One True Holy Catholic and Apostolic Church founded by St. Peter. My parents were devout. So was I. Until my mother died.

A year after my mother's death, a high-school girlfriend introduced me to Young Life, a Christian evangelical group for teens. I still grieved for my mother and was upset over a recent breakup with my boyfriend. I was a vulnerable, ideal candidate. The kids in the group seemed happy. They made me think Jesus could help me. Someday I might understand why my mother died. I became convinced that the Bible held answers to every problem and every question. When my friend told me that I was "born again," I wept and asked Jesus to be my Lord. My life began anew.

Encountering Protestant Fundamentalism

The Way followers I met in college took Young Life's message and behavior to the next level with Wierwille's dogmatic Bible classes and an agenda of influencing me to make one commitment after another. Wierwille, they said, taught people how to have a more than abundant life—only follow his teachings. I gobbled up every word.

I had not heard much, if any, Christian church history from any point of view. If I'd had, I might have understood how Wierwille was using Protestant fundamentalism for his own purposes.

Eventually, I learned that the term fundamentalism applied to

Christianity comes from a series of publications called The Fundamentals (1910–1915), which stated basic beliefs that real Christians must agree to, such as the virgin birth of Jesus, miracles, Jesus's resurrection, and biblical inerrancy. Biblical inerrancy was the foundation of Wierwille's beliefs and teachings. He explained it like this: The Bible had to be perfect because God was its author and He was perfect.

The idea of a perfect Bible as the product of a perfect God comes from trying to force logic on the Bible, not from the Bible itself. Fundamentalists such as Wierwille shove round pegs of contradictions in the Bible into the square hole of perfection to make the Bible appear without error. Rarely does anyone call them on it; their spiel is too rapid and convincing.

Wierwille's fundamentalism made sense to me when I was a teenager, given that I wanted to learn the real Word of God, not somebody's interpretation. Once introduced to Wierwille's thinking, I thought the Catholic Church had let me down since it had not insisted that the Scriptures should be the centerpiece of my faith. Young Life was great, but it had not offered in-depth Bible instruction like The Way offered. I loved God and wanted to serve Him, as the nuns had said I should, and fundamentalism disguised by Wierwille as "the accuracy of God's Word" seemed the avenue God wanted me to take to fulfill that purpose. It seemed to offer a safe, godly, and solid perch in a world swirling with confusion.

Two months after Way recruiters swept me into their cult, I dropped out of college for what became a seventeen-year commitment to the group (1970 to 1987). I was a zealous believer and eventually became a leader with unwavering loyalty. I loved my Way leaders, my Way believer friends, and most of all, the Word of God we taught. I believed, as surely as I believed the sun rose each morning, that being part of this group was God's plan for me.

I rejected every warning. A college friend warned me that Wierwille was a con man. My father told me I'd end up in the gutter. My adoring boyfriend feared Wierwille was brainwashing me. I saw these people as obstacles in my fervent pursuit of God and abandoned them for a Way-centered life.

In 1973 I graduated from The Way's two-year leadership-training program, The Way Corps, conducted at The Way headquarters property, the renovated Wierwille family farm at the edge of New Knoxville, Ohio. Supervised by Wierwille himself, our training was heavy indoctrination. We lived in trailers, worked at assigned jobs, and functioned as a unit. For those two years, I lived in one bedroom with five bunks, ten women, and one bathroom. Most of the time I loved it. Wierwille said this arrangement taught us to live together as Christians; if we couldn't learn to love each other there, then we'd have trouble helping and loving God's people when we went back into the world [after our commune-style training]. He also said that if we left, we would be turning our backs on God.

After graduation from The Way Corps, I married a man from my group, and Wierwille ordained him. For a time, we were The Way's leaders in California. We had a child. Wierwille was our "father in The Word" directing our every move. His authority was firmly planted in my mind, not only from his Bible teachings, but also from his alleged special revelation: "He [God] said He would teach me the Word as it had not been known since the first century if I would teach it to others," as he claimed in the book *The Way: Living in Love*. I had believed that assertion with all my heart. God still spoke to people today as He had in Moses' time.

I imagine now that I had wanted that so-called revelation to be true because I had been seeking correct Bible knowledge and understanding. Wierwille also claimed that his ministry was the first-century church in the twentieth century, and I trusted and followed him as the first Christians followed the Apostle Paul.

Over time, Wierwille trusted me to become one of his biblical researchers. During my Way Corps training, he assigned me to an Aramaic project. I believed this project would help us discover more of the accuracy of God's Word, which, in turn, would help believers experience more of the abundant life Jesus Christ promised.

In 1984 that powerful belief shattered like a pane of glass.

My Undoing

In August 1984, I moved with my then-husband and our daughter back to Way headquarters, our "spiritual" home. Wierwille, whom we called "our father in The Word," had retired in 1982 but still lived there, as did other leaders. By this time, about 500 staff also worked there in a massive office building—a small city under one roof. The ministry had grown into a worldwide organization with fellowships in every state in the United States and thirty-six other countries.

It was a multimillion-dollar business that received income from believers' donations, book sales, and class fees. In 1985 alone, The Way reported $30 million in income. Our goal, God's Word over the world, was becoming a reality. Thousands of Way Corps members around the globe spearheaded the movement. The Way owned other significantly large properties in Indiana, Kansas, Colorado, and Scotland, where Way Corps members were trained.

My assignment in 1984 was to help complete *The Concordance to the Peshitta Version of the Aramaic New Testament* and work on the elite Biblical Research Team that had formed in recent years. Wierwille had wanted to expand his biblical research efforts, so he'd encouraged some Way Corps graduates to attend universities and learn biblical languages to further his aims. Researchers had to be Way Corps grads first, their trustworthiness ensured, before they might be invited to join the Biblical Research Team. We were a group of about eight people from a ministry of tens of thousands.

Besides the Aramaic project, I also helped prepare weekly Bible studies. I was convinced I was doing God's will and certain Wierwille was God's chosen representative on earth until, in 1984, I began to see for myself that Wierwille fabricated and often plagiarized his biblical research and teachings. The critical instance that opened my eyes to this reality was a metaphor in Paul's epistle to the Ephesians. Over the years, Wierwille had taught that the armor described in chapter six of Ephesians was not really armor, such as soldiers wear, but instead it "had to be" athletic gear. Why? Because Wierwille said Christians were athletes of the spirit, not soldiers for the Lord. But about this context of Ephesians, he was wrong. The Greek word for *armor* really means *armor*. But because Wierwille insisted that Christians were athletes, not soldiers, he insisted on changing the text. He "spiritually knew" he was right.

I could not veer away from the fact that he was making this up. He did not acknowledge what the text actually said. I was more than baffled. I felt as if the ground broke open and a sinkhole were swallowing me. I was falling like a loose pebble. All those years, about fifteen, I had not been promoting God's Word after all. I had been propagating Wierwille's twisted interpretations.

What would I do now? I was devastated and alarmed. I had been deceived. The feeling was like that of a wife upon discovering that her husband has been cheating on her—a swirling mix of hurt, confusion, anger, and disorientation. I broke down crying, I lost sleep, I feared I could not get my emotional balance as wave after wave of realizations hit me. Wierwille was not "our father in The Word." He was the emperor with no clothes.

Wierwille's Death

Wierwille died in May 1985 while I was on the Biblical Research Team. Secretly I was glad he was dead; he could no longer hurt or confuse anyone with his twisted teachings in the service of inerrancy and himself, but soon I was shattered again when a biblical research coworker was mysteriously banished. Our leaders were fighting for power. Paranoia reigned. Murmurs of sexual abuse by leaders, weapons caches, and financial indiscretion spread. Grasping for sanity, I resigned my biblical research job, was reassigned to another department, and enrolled in a nearby college, despite veiled threats from former friends who feared I'd blow the whistle.

My Escape

My then-husband, our daughter, and I managed to escape before

I was labeled a traitor. One August morning in 1987, we fled Way headquarters before anyone discovered we'd turned our backs on the ministry. We had planned this quietly, not wanting to rouse the leaders into escorting us off the property under armed guard, as they had done with someone else who had confronted their evil doings—such as when they were conducting a secret sex ring of adultery that Wierwille had initiated. I did not want to run around the 147-acre headquarters to persuade people to leave with me. With the exception of a couple of people, the friends I had tried to talk with about research errors refused to listen. Today, some of my former friends remain in the organization, others formed offshoot ministries, and still others, like me, consider Wierwille to have been an arrogant fraud, and we've rejected him and his teachings altogether.

My Recovery
His Holiness the Dalai Lama says your religion should make you a better person. Although some good came of my association with The Way, its fundamentalist beliefs were not making me a better person. They stifled my freedom to think and speak. They usurped my creativity and funneled it into The Way's propaganda machine. They made me afraid of life because they taught that the Devil was always after me.

When I gave up The Way's teachings, I was sure I was on the right track, but I was confused about God's place in my life. My beliefs had been hammered by a switch in realities: from thinking God wanted me in The Way, to then having to reject it. I was lonely and confused, struggling to do what I thought was good for me. I was also terrified, not because I thought the Devil would ruin me for leaving The Way, but because I feared the larger world where I'd have to live and make sound decisions without the concept of a God who planned my life. I leapt off a cliff, hoping for solid ground.

Gradually I healed from having lost hundreds of friends and the certainty about God's will I'd held onto for so long. I grew more comfortable with the uncertainty of life. I finished my formal education and developed new loving friendships. Literature and philosophy helped me discern propaganda and find my own voice. Over time, I gained understanding about fundamentalism and the cult phenomenon I had experienced. Mindfulness, a meditation practice rooted in Buddhist teachings, keeps me grounded and grateful to share my story.

Reference

Whiteside, Elena S., *The Way: Living in Love.* New Knoxville, OH: American Christian Press, 1972.

V
WRITING POEMS

The First

Who knows what poetry is,
where it comes from
where it goes.

I'm not sure what it's fashioned of
or how to make it live
or if one poem is often more than one.

I do remember writing down my first, for Joey Briscoe (not his real name) in second grade:

"You're the light in my lamp,
And the bounce in my ball.
You're the glue on my stamp,
And the paint on my wall."

What is that?
A way to say Joey is
my everything?

Where did it come from?
A heart full of joy
at this blonde-haired boy.

Author's note: I wrote the above poem in the year 2000 to entertain folks who attended a reading I gave at Rollins College. At the time, I remembered only those four lines of that childhood poem for Joey that I included; it was much longer in its original form. Many years after I gave that reading, my sister found the original full-length poem among family mementos and mailed it to me. For fun, here it is in all its glory.

When your cupid shot his arrow,
It pointed right straight at me,
And here is a verse,
My cupid shot at thee.

You're the light in my lamp,
And the bounce in my ball.
You're the glue on my stamp,
And the paint on my wall.

You're the crust on my pie,
And the point on my dart,
You're the gleam in my eye,
And the key to my heart.

You're the ring in my phone,
And the rug on my floor,
You're the seat in my car,
And the bright in my day,
You're the wish on my star,
And the think of my say.

You're the jump in my hop,
And the flame in my fire,
You're the bang in my pop,
And the round in my tire.

You're the bow in my hair,
And the tune in my song.
You're the core of my pear,
And the length of my long.

You're the source of my blush,
And the thought of my think,
You're the comb with my brush,
And the roll in my rink.

You're the beat of my heart,
And the smile on my face.
You're the go of my start,
And the win of my race.

This may be a long way to say,
Be My Valentine.

Poetry and Solitude

The poet and physician William Carlos Williams (1883–1963) expressed poetry's value this way in his poem *Asphodel, That Greeny Flower & Other Love Poems*: "It is difficult / to get the news from poems / yet men die miserably every day / for lack / of what is found there." Poetry is an art form. Its condensed, image-filled language has been with us for eons, devised by skilled and inspired writers who've given—and continue giving—readers nutrients for living. For writers, poetry enters our souls, invigorates our written output, and helps us grow. What poetry have you read lately?

Two of my favorite poets are W. S. Merwin and Adrienne Rich. It's easy to check in with them regularly because I have a poem from each of them in sight of my desk: Merwin's "Place," about the sort of tree he wanted to plant on the last day of the world (one that's not born fruit yet) and Rich's poem "Delta," describing how her life flows in several directions, which I certainly relate to.

George Herbert

Let's take a few minutes to salute a rather obscure poet to most of us today: George Herbert (1593–1633). Although Herbert lived four centuries ago, he's a poet for our time … and any time. In a stanza of his poem "The Church Porch" (it's typed on a scrap of paper taped to my desk), he urges readers to engage in an activity that for writers goes with the territory.

> By all means use sometimes to be alone.
> Salute thyself: see what thy soul doth wear.
> Dare to look in thy chest, for 'tis thine own:
> And tumble up and down what thou find'st there.

Use Sometimes to Be Alone

Unlike the title of Claudia Rankine's riveting book of poetry *Don't Let Me Be Lonely: An American Lyric*, which depicts loneliness as the downer it is, "being alone" is different. It enables folks to focus their attention on the job at hand—a good thing if you're a writer. Who can write among other people who need or demand attention? No one I know of. I've never seen or heard of a writer at work in the middle of an ongoing, frenetic party. Laying out cogent sentences or dreaming up lines of poetry takes moments of undisturbed reflection, rumination, and concentration.

Another benefit of taking time out to write alone: privacy. Am I the only one who feels weird around others when I talk to myself aloud as I work? For instance, when writing a story, I might ask questions like: "No, not that word, find a synonym, will ya? Did she really say that? What was the weather like? How did that engine sound?" I don't want to inflict the rat-a-tat-tat of my questions on anyone nearby sipping coffee at 8:00 a.m. in a café. Some writers say they work well in crowded restaurants and noisy bars, but isolation, too, can be supportive when you want to "Dare to look in thy chest, for 'tis thine own." To capture spot-on words, fearless intuitions, and brilliant sentences from the ether, it often helps if we "use sometimes to be alone." And some of us just think better in silence, especially while revising.

Solitude Bears Fruit

Herbert's published work offers us the fruit of his solitary labor. The Poetry Foundation's website (Poetry.org) says:

> Herbert … did not consciously fashion an expansive literary career for himself, and his characteristic gestures, insofar as

these can be gleaned from his poems and other writings, tend to be careful self-scrutiny rather than rhetorical pronouncement; ... and complex, ever-qualified lyric contemplation rather than epic or dramatic mythmaking. This is the stuff of humility and integrity, not celebrity.

From that we can imagine, George Herbert practiced what he preached: putting into words what he discovered in his innermost self, a regular exercise that gave way to his heart-catching line, "See what thy soul doth wear."

Let's take his advice. More likely than not, we'll discover unique insights, images, and truths to share. We may even "tumble up and down" what leads to the work that Williams alluded to: life-saving. Solitude may not always be without a challenge to arrange, but carve out some time for being alone. Your inner creative writer needs it.

📖 Books I Recommend for Writing Poetry

How to Write Poetry. 2nd edition. Nancy Bogen. Macmillan General Reference. An ARCO Book. 1994.

The Practice of Poetry: Writing Exercises From Poets Who Teach. Editors: Robin Behn & Chase Twitchell.

The Poet's Dictionary: A Handbook of Prosody and Poetic Devices by William Packard.

Poetic Meter & Poetic Form by Paul Fussell.

Goatfoot, Milktongue, Twinbird: Interviews, Essays, and Notes on Poetry, 1970-76 by Donald Hall.

The Demon and the Angel: Searching for the Source of Artistic Inspiration by Edward Hirsch, author of *How to Read a Poem.*

Sound and Sense: An Introduction to Poetry (Seventh Edition) by Laurence Perrine.

More of Charlene's Poems

Migration

Painted bird formation
   on watercolor paper, small, stiff,
     swollen with paint,
     formed in a burst of wings,
  a hint of its journey
woven on parchment.

Hands made from dust itself
   shaped lapis birds held silent
    filled with indigo visions.
   A flight stilled on
fibrous compression.

One soaring spirit,
   settled in an artist,
     moved through flesh,
captured migration.

In Secret

I learned it's best to pray
or fast or offer alms in private—
in church pews or darkened cells far from view.

"Do those things alone and in silence," I heard—
like hidden cats kneading fallen sweaters,
offering up strange animal psalms.

Matches

The satin cover stained with rust and mold
with curved gold letters held the names and date.
November twenty-six still legible,
I wonder what they'd say to that today?

Its white turned yellow now that it is old,
perhaps the bride's dress, too, has darkened some.
To think this many years have come and gone,
now where is she, Patricia and her Charles?

The matchbook lay innocuous and soft,
I opened it to find one small gray stub—
where someone tore that match to light a wick?
Or when Charles lit her cigarette in bed?

Tucked in their dresser drawer, it spent these years
'til someone cleaned the drawer and cleared away
the matchbook with two wedding bells and names—
a token left behind of love-lit days.

Chowchilla, California: July 15, 1976

For Joan Brown and her children

In 1825 Mexican explorers in the San Joaquin valley
thirsted and died in the Chowchilla riverbed.
The river alternately flows and dries through this California,

careless with death, it divides the town, Chowchilla.
Those days, like tattered photographs, have faded from view.
Civilization smoothed the rough "old days" over.

In 1976 a killer-spirit swept through.
Three outsiders raided the valley—
kidnappers, soul-thieves who stole Chowchilla's young ones,
took their school bus off the road.

Parents' frantic prayers flew like paper napkins
grabbed by gusts of wind.
Police sifted through every clue; every lead tied to possible life.

Why did they take our children?

The question, ancient as Cain,
only three men could answer
who'd funneled the terrified
into a buried truck.

Twenty-six children, entombed,
clung to tears and skin.
Hours and air seeped away.
Some gagged on the stench of excrement.
Death, their guardian, waited against the wall.

Then a song.
The captives dared to sing,
as if a universal language might save them.
Soon, small fingers found a tiny crack and scraped a way to life—
as crocuses push through softened earth
children climbed out into a red and swollen world.

Author's Note: Joan Brown and I worked together in Tampa, Florida, 1996-98. She told me her horrifying story, loaned me a book about it, then I wrote this poem for her.

Tears

In 2001, after eye surgery,
the doctor said, "Use these artificial tears
if you need to."
He handed me a small, sealed bottle.
I put it on a shelf and waited.

That was Monday,
one day after I packed the belongings
of my terminally ill friend,
watched her drive off
to another town with hope
of a new doctor's cure.

The bottled tears stayed on the shelf
unopened, unneeded.

That was Monday,
one day before September eleventh.

Fly, Woman-Child, Fly

For Rachel, my daughter

The river between us, wide one minute, ribbon the next,
Dares me to cross, to carry you back.

You, woman-child, stand firm, a silhouette in blue.
From this side, I see arrows in your heart
where roses used to be, but
you persist despite them.

You, woman-child, touch waters, sound the depths,
note currents swirling at your feet.
Will sodden riverbeds hold you?
Will the silver air?

Stretch open your hands, woman-child
aching to fly—a heron who eyes the stream,
legs as spindles under your weight.
Sun multiplies your wings in mirrored rivulets.

When you were small, I saw from a window
you in a yellow sunsuit, straddled on the rim
of the sandbox, a plastic spoon raised mid-air, as if
deciding whether to toss it or dig in.

Your mouth then—under the softest eyes on earth—
too young to speak with glorious insight, yet
your very being in this act spoke tomes, charmed me,
dearest one, to keep on.

Later, I had bags of pebbles, each marked with an answer.
With them, we built towers in the stream.
They've tumbled in a rush of water and of time.
Go with caution. Fly when you can.

Encounters

*For survivor Hoyt, my husband,
who dreams and dares*

Maxine Kumin writes of animals—
their habits, needs and wants.
Like humans, the wild ones spend
five senses and hidden powers to survive.

Surviving, you're with me at the table.
Our food is spread before us:
bread and cheese and wine.

I learn you are a man truly spared.
Five lions gave you up one African night,
your jeep stuck in spinning sand.
Unmoving in your seat, you think:
The End.   It's been a good life.

I think of Maxine's poem,
"Encounter in August" –
a bear stole into her camp,
looked her in the face,
ate her beans,
lumbered back into the wild.

Your lions spread themselves atop the road,
dazed and gorged by the bloody kill,
too poor-sighted to understand
the difference between machine and man.

Their eyes glowed in steady headlights
while you surveyed memories spread before you
like bread and cheese and wine.

Jungle kings, dazed and weary,
satisfied and dull,
sauntered back into the wild.

On mornings as I wake with you
I thank them.

VI
WRITING STORIES

Writing a Very Short Story

What story is really worth writing? Worth spending your time, energy, and imagination on? I like what Susan Sontag says in *As Consciousness Is Harnessed to Flesh*, "The only story that seems worth writing is a cry, a shot, a scream. A story should break the reader's heart." Whenever I read Sontag's quote, what comes to mind is *flash fiction*. It's bite-size insight. It's sudden. It surprises. It's short.

What's Flash Fiction?
Whatever you call a brief piece of prose. It is shorter than a conventional short story and its brevity links it to narrative poetry. Put another way, it's a mash-up of short story and poetry. Flash fiction tends to be one to five pages long (some editors prefer it to be 1,000 or fewer words). Make each word as specific as it can be. For instance, rather than *church*, use *chapel, cathedral,* or *prayer hut*. Seek out strong adjectives, e.g. "The dilapidated prayer hut." Delete any adverbs unless they are crucial to your story. (Some folks say cut all adverbs forever. I say use them sparingly and with great discretion.) Name colors, sounds, smells, and feelings, the air and the weather, the light and the darkness. Involve as many of the five senses as is appropriate. Waste no words.

To keep you at it, if you're looking for a writing motto, I suggest: "Focus, focus, focus, and practice, practice, practice." Also, get as much feedback from your peers as you can. And offer some on their work, too. This is critical to improving your work, but I know it's not always easy, is it? But without focus, without practice, without getting some helpful responses to your work, writing gets sloppy, mistake-riddled, and weak. Stay strong.

A Book about Flash Fiction

Here's a little story about a book. In 1988—yeah, ancient times—I took a creative writing class. Our teacher assigned us a book about composing these very short stories. Although I don't have what I wrote, I do still have that book: *Sudden Fiction: American Short-Short Stories*, edited by Robert Shapard and James Thomas. One of my favorite stories in it is Robert Kelly's "Rosary." It opens with:

> Here is a man walking on a road under the half-moon. The trees are tall and well-furred; the light is little. In his left hand, sometimes swinging at his side and sometimes held lightly poised over his heart, he counts the crystal beads of a rosary. After a quarter of a mile of dark road, he passes a large building of some hard to determine kind.

Hooked? I was. The entire story is only one page long. It has an O. Henry ending, meaning it stops with a twist.

Sudden Fiction was published thirty-three years ago, but what it offers is as fresh as a Florida rainstorm rendering tropical plants bright green. The book showcases fabulous work from Grace Paley, John Cheever, Roy Blount, John Updike, Mary Robison, and Tobias Wolff, to name a few. I love what Robert Shapard says about these works in his introduction:

> The name short-short story may be relatively new, but its forms are as old as parable and fable, myth and exemplum…. These works exist regardless of any name we give them, and thoughtful readers have always known that the essence of story lies little with theory and not at all in length—Randall Jarrell

has noted that stories can be as short as a sentence—but in wishes, dreams, and sometimes truth.

📖 Books I Recommend for Writing Stories

Flash! Writing the Very Short Story by John Dufresne

Turning Life into Fiction: Finding Character, Plot, Setting and Other Elements of Novel and Short Story Writing in the Everyday World by Robin Hemley

Sudden Fiction: American Short-Short Stories, edited by Robert Shapard and James Thomas

New Sudden Fiction: Short-Short Stories from America and Beyond, edited by Robert Shapard and James Thomas

How Fiction Works by James Wood

"From the Porch" (a Short-Short Story)

The following is one of my short-short stories. Melanie Craven, the main character, also appears later in this guidebook in **Part X: More Melanie Stories**.

Melanie Craven stood on the porch, pouring salted nuts into a bowl, when the doorbell rang. She knew it must be Loretta. She met this woman only a week earlier at a friend's party, and the very next day surprised herself by calling Loretta to invite her over for a drink and a chat. Initiating something like this with a brand-new acquaintance brought her some discomfort, but she was desperate for a particular kind of company. She imagined this Saturday evening with Loretta would offer boundless relief, an evening of camaraderie filled with warm encouragement—the opposite of her day job working for a glad-handing salesman. In three seconds flat, Melanie made it from the porch to the door: Loretta had arrived.

Loretta was a world apart from Melanie's boss: a rotund man with a pockmarked face whose typical morning greeting was, "Listen up! I've got another great idea!" Whenever Melanie heard that, she shrank in despair, knowing it was a fairly reliable sign of an impending mess. The result? Needless work for her. To recover on weekends, she slid out of that harness of chaos and practiced writing, not to benefit the marketplace but to actualize her dream: to be a *real* writer. She wrote stories and poems, and like millions of others, fantasized about writing a novel. At the party, other guests gave her the impression that

Loretta was a respected, experienced writer; she seemed adored by many, important to know. Maybe she possessed writing secrets Melanie craved to learn. Perhaps this accomplished person would share one or two of those secrets that might open paths of understanding and success. And it's true. That night on the porch Loretta would divulge a significant secret, but not the kind Melanie hoped for.

* * *

Melanie felt lucky to have found this apartment with a porch. The apartment, 1920s style, had ten-foot ceilings, wooden floors, and a cozy breakfast nook. Almost every morning at 5:30 a.m. before driving to work, she stumbled to her nook and scribbled in her journal, just as her writing professors had advised: they said her sleepy subconscious would give her images she could clothe in meaning for stories and poems. Sometimes she did her half-conscious scribbling out on the porch. That screened-in room was the main reason she'd rented this place. Its screens were floor-to-ceiling; a hanging fan gave off a hypnotizing hum; although the porch was small, it had enough room for a little plastic table and two chairs—pale green wooden Adirondack chairs, slung low but supportive.

* * *

At the front door, the women exchanged friendly greetings, tinged with a little awkwardness, then trailed through the small living room and the open French doors to the porch where Melanie offered the nuts with red or white wine. She gestured to stemmed glasses on the table.

Loretta frowned. "Not just now." She waved off her hostess and sank into one of the Adirondacks. "Actually, I brought something else." She held up a slim brown paper bag. "Sit down and take a load off, dear, and we can have drinks in a minute. What a great little place you have." Melanie thanked her and sat in the other chair. She loved being on this porch, or any porch: half-inside, half-outside. There, she gained or regained perspective. There, she restored her weary self. A porch meant rest. Its arrangement, situated between protective indoors and airy outdoors, reflected the way she considered her existence: half inside herself (or maybe more than half) and the rest of herself out in the world. Behind the gossamer screens, she spent hours and hours with her various thoughts and many books, in the company of nearby hoot owls, a floor lamp shining over her shoulder. The evening she finished reading Virginia Woolf's *A Room of One's Own*, she wept—right there on the porch.

From below, honeysuckle vines along the chain-link fence puffed wafts of perfume through the air even to the third floor where they were. A car rolled quietly down the street in front of the building's trim grassy lawn.

"Great to relax on a perch, er, a porch like this," Loretta gave a sly smile, her eyes twinkling. A lanky woman, she seemed folded like a letter into the chair. She wore dark pants and a no-nonsense white blouse with blue stripes; horn-rimmed glasses framed her narrow face; silvery hair lay neatly cut in a bob. For a minute, she surveyed the street as if she owned it, her legs stretched out, her sighs loud enough to hear. "Now," she began, turning towards her hostess, "I'm ready for a nip. You too?" She pulled a bottle of bourbon from the bag. Melanie said sure, although she didn't much like bourbon. At the sight of the amber bottle, worry shot through her, but she held to the hope of discovering how Loretta dared to live the independent artist's life that Virginia Woolf described. At least she imagined Loretta did.

What she'd heard of this woman's history surely intrigued her. For one thing, Loretta had written for a local television station. That sounded challenging and probably educational, depending on the stories she covered. Even though Melanie didn't yearn to do that, wouldn't it be insightful and full of lessons? But even better, her party-organizer friend had whispered once that Loretta wrote literary stories on the side too.

Loretta poured bourbon into two recycled jam jars—Melanie had hurriedly retrieved them from the kitchen—and from a can she carried in a coat-length sweater pocket, she added a few splashes of cola. "Cheers," the women said in unison, and clinked their sturdy glass jars.

They sipped the biting whiskey and traded get-to-know-me facts about where they grew up, what foods they liked, what kinds of books they read and so on, and soon Loretta unwound, warmed by the bourbon. She also warmed up from having a rapt audience, one who seemed to look up to her. Soon, more of her history came spilling out like red, blue, and yellow plastic toys tumbling from a tipped-over box.

Melanie sighed, overwhelmed by the monologue, unable to voice any questions remotely related to any kind of writing: journalistic, business, or literary. Nearby streetlights blinked on and illuminated the older writer's wrinkled, yet animated face; her captive audience remained curled in her chair.

"Okay, Melanie, dear, now … a juicy secret I've never told anyone, not even my boys. Promise you'll keep it zipped."

Melanie promised. She'd met Loretta's adult sons at that party, and since they lived across the country, it was highly unlikely she'd ever see them again. This was an easy vow to keep.

"Before I married Jack, the boys' father," Loretta sighed, "I was married to someone else."

Melanie nodded respectfully, sipped the bourbon, and blinked a few times, not shocked by this revelation but a little surprised. She'd met Jack at the party, too: an unsmiling man who held his cocktail glass so firmly his knuckles were white.

"Now, Sam—that's my first husband's name—what a control freak he was, and I knew he was like that from the beginning, but he had a wild side too and was exciting and I was terribly in love. *Terribly.* I had it really bad. Thought he did too from the way he chased me around, especially after the ten o'clock news. We both worked at the largest TV station in town. In those days I wrote news reports, even weather stuff if you can believe that. But behind the scenes, I dreamt of being a big-time author, wrote some stories … hardly ever got any published. Rejection slips, sky high. Dang it. So, I gave up, dug in at the station and even took on some writing for radio programs and wrote speeches for local politicians. I made a little money, really little. I had an efficiency apartment, and an old VW Beetle my dad gave me when I graduated from college. Oh yeah, I can tell you I had some pretty wild times out drinking with my gal pals on the weekends."

Loretta took a long sip, then added, "What crazy days those were." She scooped a couple of cashews from the bowl, gobbled them up. Appearing to squint in deepest thought, she tilted her head in Melanie's direction. "You know, dear, you remind me of myself a little bit when I had high hopes and stars in my eyes about being a writer. A famous one. At least a published one. Your friend who threw the party told me that was your dream. It's a fine one, don't get me wrong, but you still gotta pay the bills, right? It's hard to write literary stuff while you're a workaday gal, and it gets crazy chasing after editors and waiting for agents to take or reject you and impressing publishers and all that tiresome business that wannabe writers freak out about or don't even *know* about when they say they think they want to be a writer, not to mention all the rewriting and revising and abandoning stories and changing points of view and all the upsetting days and nights and bad dreams that go with it."

Melanie gulped her drink. She was too tongue-tied to respond, and the bourbon was getting to her. She just sat waiting for more colorful and long-winded details about Loretta's convoluted writing life, her flashy past, and her lover boy, which were sure to come.

"So, about two years after college, when I was still chasing after copyeditors and agents, and about two months after I met Sam, we went to the courthouse, slipped rings on our fingers, and honeymooned in Key West. Yep, drove all the way the hell down there, speeding like a ski boat atop that peacock-blue water. Stayed in a pretty swanky hotel and strolled Duval from end to end. Watched that glorious orange-red sunset from Mallory Square with about fifty other gawkers, our mouths hanging open. Ran around to all the bars. Absolutely stuffed ourselves with shrimp and grouper dripping in butter and later smashed blue crabs—the sweetest crabs anywhere—and pigged out 'til midnight. Gobbled all that seafood right out of the nets, washed it down with gallons of chardonnay and daiquiris—of course, love that rum—and you know Sloppy Joe's is there, Papa Hemingway's hangout. Right? His work enamored me back then. Now I think he is a little too chop-chop. Don't you?"

Melanie nodded, but didn't bring herself to admit she hadn't read Hemingway. Instead, she drained her jam jar. *Bam.* A car door slammed across the street. She tipped forward to watch her matronly neighbor, who'd just gotten out of her banged-up Ford, walk slowly toward her sagging white cottage. On her head was the wide-brimmed hat she always wore: plain brown, no flowers. From this angle, she looked like a mushroom bobbing her way up the steps. In a plodding whiskey haze, Melanie feared she'd end up like that: old and alone and unpublished and un-famous and un ...

"Halloo, calling Melanie! Come on back here, girl!"

Melanie jerked her attention back to Key West.

"So," the older woman said, flicking a strand of gray hair out of her eyes, "after we got back from the Keys, Sam, as fun as he was, had a little too much fun with the secretary from the newsroom, and one night we fought like hell about it." Loretta leaned over to the little table, grabbed the bottle, and poured more bourbon into their jam jars. She ignored the cola.

"Parted ways on exactly the one-hundredth day of that mad and lusty fling. One hundred days on the dot. On the dot! Ran back to the courthouse and got that marriage annulled, baby, as in 'it never happened,' and I'll never let on to the boys. No sirree. Some things you just never tell."

After Loretta left, Melanie returned to her Adirondack for a while, staring into the vacant green chair beside her. Shadows played within the streetlight's faint glow; a hoot owl sent a gentle call through the trees. Perhaps, she wondered, any secrets to success in the writerly life (if they existed at all) were like obscure short-lived marriages: rarely revealed and things she'd simply have to figure out herself.

Chameleon One

Numbers blink one, two, three…
… ten shudders stopped.
Doors swish aside,
top floor meets my feet.
I have reached the pinnacle—
my cubicle awaits!

Chameleon one,
turned bright to pale.
Camo green, yellow, creamy brown
fading.
Dim the tones.
Be another's color now.
Dull the green.
Mute the yellow muse.
Put on brown yes-man hues.
Convert to minion.
Turn outside in
with a flick
of survival's palette,

camouflage pigment
by pigment cell
till dullest shades
fill marketplace demands.

VII
TRAVEL WRITING

With Dragons

On the borders of old maps
cartographers painted: "Here be dragons,"
warning those who landed there—

either deliberately or
having been mistaken;
out of fear or
having no other choice.

But for some, to stay within the borders
is more certain a destruction
than taking chances with the monsters.

See now, the dark green water in the distance?
Hear the creature stirring in the deep?
Find me there.
Shall we dip and soar astride it?

Writing Meaningful Travel Stories

Whether you've journeyed to Key West or the Far East, your travels are unique. Your stories about them are, too, and can appeal to readers near or not so nearby. Lots of folks want to experience vicarious travel. They'd love to find out about another place from someone who can communicate their experience in an ordered and interesting way. Would you like to give those readers that chance?

Traveler or Tourist?
Travel stories of depth differ from travel blogs, like ones about *What I Did on My Summer Vacation* (on Monday we went to the museum, saw stuffed dinosaurs, ate hamburgers, etc.). They differ from guidebooks for tourists, too, that suggest what to see, where to stay, what to eat, and what to be sure not to miss. While you may describe those details in your stories, the kind I'm talking about reads less like a travel guide and more like a memoir or novel. It's your *true-life* story about your travel adventures, whether you visited a different place for a brief time or lived there for a while.

Travel writing aims to relay something uniquely meaningful to you, perhaps even life changing. In turn, it offers readers a journey beyond their comfort zone.

Sources to Get Your Travel Story Moving
For more than twenty years, my husband and I have travelled to dis-

tant lands. I've written journals, emails, and blog posts about many of those experiences and taken tons of photographs of these journeys. If you've kept that kind of documentation from your travel explorations, it's the primary source material for your writing project. Start there.

With a yellow highlighter and your journal, mark sentences that jump out at you: they may point you toward specific theme(s). Drag out those boxes of postcards, brochures, and mementos from the back of the closet. Maybe sort them in piles by topic. Comb through your photos; hunt to find especially unusual ones to draw readers into your story. Study those photos to bring back memories of landscapes, sounds, and colors. Relive the smells and look of unique foods you tasted. Reflect on your transportation challenges and how you solved them (or not) and the memorable people you met. I think of the couple from the US that my husband and I encountered on a street in Hanoi, Vietnam, who helped us with directions: they were professionals working at the American embassy who happened to be out jogging that sweltering afternoon. In other words, rev up your travel engine senses to get your story moving.

Keep Nonfiction Travel Writing Simple

Keep it simple. Convey just one aspect of your trip. For instance, relay a serendipitous event that features the kindness of strangers like the one we had in Hanoi, above. Here's another of mine on that topic. A drugstore clerk in Shanghai, China, was unable to understand my desperate need for a bottle of Vitamin C—I had a terrible cold. I didn't speak a word of Chinese. Even with my best game-of-charades gestures, I failed to communicate. After a few moments of confusion, the clerk called to someone far back in the stockroom. That person, we learned, was her adult daughter. She came to the counter and told me she also worked in a hospital, which had given her the chance to learn some English. What luck for me. Her mother could have waved me away—a confused and annoying American tourist. Instead, she took pity and helped this foreign stranger. Her thoughtfulness brought lots of smiles and gratitude and made a lasting memory. Incidents like that show the loveliness in humanity. They give us hope.

Pick a Corner of the Planet
William Zinsser in *On Writing Well: An Informal Guide to Writing Nonfiction*, points out:

> … Nobody can write a book or an article "about" something. Even Tolstoy couldn't write a book about war and peace, or Melville a book about whaling. They made certain reductive decisions about time and place and about individual characters in that time and place. Every writing project must be reduced before you start to write it. Therefore, think small. Decide what corner of your subject you're going to bite off, and be content to cover it well, and stop.

Describe in Full
In Jack Heffron's *The Writer's Idea Book: How to Develop Great Ideas for Fiction, Nonfiction, Poetry, & Screenplays*, he offers prompts galore (more than 400) to kick off your writing sessions. Here's one about place:

> Write about the best place you've ever been. "Best" can have a few meanings: most exciting, most fulfilling, most interesting.… Take time to describe it in detail.… After you have a few pages of description, you can begin to explain and speculate upon why this place had such a profound impact on you.

Dig into your heart and sift through your travel memories. Select one to describe in full. Reflect on why you found your time there, at that place, meaningful to *you*. Universal appeal for readers usually turns up in specific, personal incidents—they reveal your vulnerability, a relatable human trait.

Vulnerable Traveler—Humanizing Story or Poem
A way to get personal is to imagine yourself telling a dear friend about

your travels. She absolutely craves a vicarious travel experience. You know your friend loves you and that confidence eases you into revealing more of the emotions and insights you had during and after your escapades. Include as many details as you can to engage her. Use strong adjectives, like "the cantankerous hotel manager." Tell your friend the effect travel had on you. Be honest. "When I got home, I was grateful for the trip, but I was totally exhausted." Be thoughtful. Gustave Flaubert shared this soul-enriching effect: "Travel makes one modest. You see what a tiny place you occupy in the world."[6]

P.S. Your story may call out to take the form of poetry rather than prose. A trip to Greece in the summer of 2001 with my then-future husband, Hoyt, inspired "Gadfly," included after this reading list.

📖 Books I Recommend for Travel Writing

The Mindful Traveler: A Guide to Journaling and Transformative Travel by Jim Currie.

Better Than Fiction: True Travel Tales from Great Fiction Writers. Don George, Editor.

The Best American Travel Writing 2020. Robert Macfarlane, Editor. Series editor: Jason Wilson (other years are also available).

Deep South: Four Seasons on Back Roads (2015) by Paul Theroux was described by Kirkus Reviews in a starred review as "an epically compelling travel memoir."

The Travel Writer's Handbook: How to Write—and Sell—Your Own Travel Experiences by Louise Purwin Zobel and Jacqueline Harmon Butler.

---

[6] https://www.goodreads.com/quotes/76288-travel-makes-one-modest-you-see-what-a-tiny-place.

Gadfly

For my husband, Hoyt L. Edge

No rain for us ... in sweat at the Parthenon
where sunburned tourists like ourselves
huddle by worn-out guides, strain to hear
mysteries whispered past columns,
over scarlet-veined marble beneath our feet.

I look down and your shadow blends
into mine on the dust-covered ground.
I wonder aloud who walked here
thousands of years ago.
We remember Socrates, the good-trouble maker.

Further along, we sight atop another hill
a tavern, decrepit in its ancient place.
You, my philosopher-man, hold the guidebook,
study with ease lengthy descriptions.

The keeper at a corner shop says, yes, yes, oh yes,
that's exactly where they imprisoned
that old Gadfly, delivered him his poison.

You grin and we commence toward the hill
only to find scaffolding in our way.
You breach a sagging caution tape and there
on a blue chair at a blue table with other blue ones
piled about, you mime The Gadfly
at the table, drinking, drinking.

Writing Behind the Scenes in Kas, Turkey

> *"Secretly we spoke, that wise one and me.*
> *I said, 'Tell me the secrets of the world.'*
> *He said, 'Sssh, let silence tell you the secrets of the world.'"*
> —Rumi, mystic poet and founder of the
> Whirling Dervishes whose burial place is in Konya, Turkey

While in Turkey 2011, my husband, Hoyt, and I spent a night in the town of Kas, a delightful fishing village on the azure Mediterranean Sea.

Kas was an idyllic spot to land in, muse, rest, and write. Seafood tasted salty and delicious, especially the fried calamari, which I love. We were on the last leg of our month-long journey through the ancient history-laden land once called Asia Minor, and I had a lot to say about the trip. I took extensive notes while traveling. When we returned home, I wrote a detailed travel blog about our Turkey adventures titled "From the Edge in Turkey."[7]

That vacation truly fascinated and educated me about ancient history, art, and archeology, but writing about it was not a holiday. Although it wasn't in the category of a travel story described in the previous essay, "Writing Meaningful Travel Stories," it still required detailed work.

---

[7] You can read it and enjoy the accompanying photographs at: http://charleneedge-turkey2011.blogspot.com.

On the cover of this guidebook is a photo Hoyt took of me on the porch of The Hideaway Hotel where we stayed in Kas. I'm mulling things over, considering what to write: my journal lies ready on the table in front of me. I look to the sea, as if searching for words to capture how I feel. I love that kind of time before the actual writing of anything. It's like puttering around in a garden for images and metaphors. It's akin to whiling away an hour in that garden, mindlessly pulling out a weed, inhaling the rainy smell of earth, taking pleasure in a little brown bird who hops up to you for a closer look.

Actual Writing

The actual writing about the trip was a difficult blogging experience, but I'm not complaining, just sayin'. Planning, writing, rewriting, deleting, rearranging, and coffee drinking. Enjoyable, yes, for the most part, but work just the same. It took me about three steady weeks full-time to construct the organization of the blog and shape its content. (I took time off from working on what would years later become *Undertow*.)

Have you heard this joke? At a cocktail party, a surgeon is chatting with a writer. The surgeon says, "Yeah, I think I'll take a weekend off and write a novel." The writer says, "Yeah, I think I'll take a weekend off and do brain surgery."

That blog was brain surgery for me. It's the most extensive recapture that I've written of any trip we've taken, and I probably won't do anything like it again. I'd rather shift to writing travel *stories*.

Persistence

The blog about Turkey taught me, once again, that when it comes to writing anything, even a postcard, persistence is "The Little Engine that Could." You might remember that children's story. Persistence, devotion, and love, I read somewhere, make things happen. Without them, I could not write this. Without those qualities in the writers who have gone before us, what writer among us would try this work with any sense that it matters?

My Unscientific Theories

The other day, a friend, who is a marvelous editor, reminded me that each word carries a nuance. We have so many to choose from. Why settle for "nice" when "agreeable," "pleasant," or "lovely" are waiting to speak up, ready to go?

Nuance is like a facet of a diamond, one of the multiple planes on a cut gem's surface. Turn an idea this way and that until the light strikes the right facet, and *wham!* You know you've found exactly what you wanted to say.

I make up theories like that, just ask my husband. Here's another: when the right word comes along for a writer, it resonates with something mysterious inside us, like a wind chime clanging in response to a breeze. Put another way, the right words slide like puzzle pieces into the pattern of the larger work. Perhaps, in part, that "something mysterious" has to do with all the reading the writer has done. The reading is a storehouse of emotion, vocabulary, metaphors, units of meaning, all made of words. Fling those storehouse doors wide open.

Master Authors

The author, essayist, and environmental advocate, Barry Lopez, impressed me when he conducted a Master Class at Rollins College in 2010.[8] I took notes. One point he made about writers is that they are pattern makers.

"That's why we write," he said. "What kind of patterns do we want to weave?"

I would like to see more threads of empathy and independence woven into patterns that writers weave. I see them within Lopez's work. My favorite book of his, *Resistance,* is a novel told from nine points of view about creative people who resisted the status quo … and persecution.

---

[8] While putting together this guidebook, I was shocked to learn that on Christmas Day, 2020, our wonderful Barry Lopez passed away. Among many honors, in February 2020, he was elected to the American Academy of Arts and Letters. "In Memoriam" messages are posted on his website: https://barrylopez.com.

The *San Francisco Chronicle* review, cited on the back cover of my copy of *Resistance*, reads: "Lopez has ventured out into territory quite risky and raised important questions ... that few other fiction writers have made stick."

Patterns reveal a deliberate order. Moving words around until they settle in the right places on the page is the writer's labor to make order out of chaos. Shuffling or replacing words may sound like a weird task to do voluntarily, yet something makes us want to craft a tapestry out of human experience, hang it on the wall as a unified piece that makes sense, makes beauty, makes, as Barry says, "a pattern of grace."

We aim to find Cinderella and deliver that glass slipper.

Annie Dillard, another writer I admire, says many wise and wonderful things in her book *The Writing Life*. One bit I like is: "Only after the writer lets literature shape her can she perhaps shape literature."

She also remarks on what a privilege it is "to muck about in sentences all morning."

Disclaimer

You can be sure of this: I do not consider my ramblings here anything close to literature, but some day, in some way, I might accomplish what Annie describes. One thread after another. One glass slipper after another. Oops: we mustn't mix metaphors like I just did, but ... this is not literature.

VIII

KEEP MOVING / INSPIRATION

Letter to the Editors

(Best read aloud and very fast.)

So, what the hell do you want?

I sent you my blood my

earliest morning journal entries

I mailed you my workshopped-to-death essays

and final exams rewritten you got my

poems I know you did those babies I

barely can let go of they spill my

guts and glory so what the hell else can you

possibly expect from someone

who works 40 hours a week not

counting the 45-minute drive down the

interstate and what about the half-hour

lunches crammed with speed reading the latest issue of Poets and Writers

magazine devouring the poems by the

famous names and once in a while an unknown

first-timer but I doubt that honest I do I

sent another batch out yesterday on the heels of your

enigmatic rejection letter which by the way was

so clever and witty congratulations on your

creativity in writing this is just to say we

have taken some plums we found in our

mailbox you were hoping they would be yours
forgive us others seemed sweeter or colder or
bolder or whatever yeah whatever of course there was
no evidence of a human sending this note to me no
signature sealed the deal no one would admit to
rejecting yet another poor delusional soul no one
had a precious second to scribble an initial I would've
taken a frowny face so how do I know you
are editors posing as humans so really do you expect
me to believe you a friend told me she received a
rejection slip from an editor to whom she
HADN'T EVEN SENT ANYTHING she
said it was like taking a walk down a lovely street and
having someone open a door and yell out you
can't come in I laughed till I cried and
peed in my pants when I heard that one so
that's what you're really up to so what you really
want after all is to beat me to it so if that's what you
want then that's what you'll get so go
ahead and send that slip before I send you
anything I'll show you!

Writing a Moment of Being

Virginia Woolf strikes a pose—in my imagination. She looms large in many writers' minds as a genius author, a grand maker of memoir, of fiction, a most significant literary figure of the twentieth century. She was a founding member of the famed soiree "Bloomsbury Group," a mix of writers, philosophers, intellectuals, and artists who regularly shared their work and lives in a part of London called Bloomsbury. I imagine it as a writers' critique group on steroids.

Moments of Being

Whether we are part of a writers' group or not, I think we all hope to improve our craft by learning from others. One way to do this is to take a little time to read and study highly creative and astute authors like Virginia Woolf. Years ago, I bought a slim volume of her work titled *A Room of One's Own,* which primarily advocates for women to claim the time and space they need for their writing work. Gee, here we are in the twenty-first century, and this topic is still highly relevant.

Later, I read *Virginia Woolf: Moments of Being*. It is a collection of Woolf's memoir pieces that were discovered after her death in 1941, edited by Jeanne Schulkind, and first published in 1976. What *are* moments of being? Woolf describes them as bits of time when we feel intense emotion, when something superbly significant captures our attention, and we are compelled to create a meaning *for* it, to associate meanings *with* it, to *remember* it. Those moments *stay* with us. I daresay that for writers, after such moments we cannot but ruminate about them, write them down, examine their qualities, dive into them for treasures we can assign meaning to. We find ourselves expressing those moments on the page to fix them in time and place, like a portrait in a frame. Maybe we include them in our own memoir pieces. Maybe we make moments like that shine in the life of a new character we develop for a novel or short story. Or include them in a poem. Pivotal moments. Moments of life in full tilt.

What about Non-Being?
Sometimes it is useful to describe a thing in terms of what it is *not*, to clarify that "something." I think a good way to communicate Woolf's thoughts about *being* and *non-being* is to let her tell you herself from a section of that book, *Moments of Being*:

> Often when I have been writing one of my so-called novels, I have been baffled by ... how to describe what I call in my private shorthand: "non-being." Every day includes much more non-being than being. Yesterday for example, Tuesday the 18th of April, was [as] it happened a good day; above the average in "being." It was fine; I enjoyed writing these first pages; my head was relieved of the pressure of writing about Roger; I walked over Mount Misery and along the river; and save that the tide was out, the country, which I notice very closely always, was coloured and shaded as I like—there were the willows, I remember, all plumy and soft green and purple against the blue.... These separate moments of being were however embedded in many more moments of non-being. I have already forgotten what Leonard and I talked about at lunch; and at tea; although it was a good day the goodness was embedded in a kind of nondescript cotton wool. This is always so. A great part of every day is not lived consciously. One walks, eats, sees things, deals with what has to be done; the broken vacuum cleaner;

cooking dinner.... When it is a bad day the proportion of non-being is much larger.

Cotton Wool vs. Consciousness

I love that phrase Woolf uses to describe humdrum everyday actions and thoughts like when we open mail, set appointments, pay bills, houseclean, drive cars—*cotton wool*. Maybe I should speak for only myself here, but don't we often go through parts of our days in a fog, on automatic at a slug's pace, and maybe even half asleep? Woolf calls us out for this: "a great part of every day is not lived consciously." Okay, Virginia, I admit that's true for me. But I'm not sure any human being could live 100 percent consciously every single minute of every single day. However, I do want to ask myself and other writers what might happen if we made a serious attempt to decrease the cotton wool in our days and increase moments of conscious living—*moments of being*? What might happen to our writing?

Cut Loose: Walk, Think, Write

Calling all writers—get out. Stroll, pace, or wander. We give the page a piece of our mind, let's give our bodies a push out the door. Even a quick fifteen-minute walk can reward you with unexpected writerly gifts. Now, I understand that for some of us, this is not an option, that environmental or safety issues make a leisurely walk outdoors prohibitive. But for those of us who can get out there, let's not take it for granted.

Sever the Familiar for a Time

It's no secret that a change of scenery is good for our mental and physical health. If we live in the city, let's see if we can find a nearby park. The fresh air can often lift our spirits, improve our outlook, and increase our appreciation of nature.

Experiment. Cut yourself free from your familiar writing space and take a quick walk, even into another room. Look out the window, or better yet, open the door and get outside and soak in some Vitamin D. To engage in a walk, especially in areas where trees, plants, and birds live, is one way to loosen up your writing muscles and relieve neck and shoulder tension (a writer's plague, indeed). It offers practice in paying attention to our body's movements and our mind's ruminations. Many writers, like Henry David Thoreau, extolled the virtues of walking as a tonic for a person's soul *and* for stories. As Thoreau wrote in his journal, "Me thinks that the moment my legs begin to move, my thoughts begin to flow."

Give Your Writing Some Fresh Air

On a personal note, while I was writing the complicated manuscript that became my memoir *Undertow*, brisk walks in my neighborhood calmed me. They were (and still are) a mental health necessity. They gave me a break to try different ideas too. Walking alone, I shook off the dust of frustration, breathed deeply, and opened myself to new thoughts about my work. I reflected on ways to be more innovative with scene construction, portray abstract ideas more effectively through dialogue, and organize chapters. And more than once, I coaxed myself down off that familiar ledge called "I must be crazy for trying to write at all!"

Leave Your Earbuds at Home

Instead of listening to music through earbuds, listen to real, live songbirds. Observe the color of clouds, other people on the street, how cool or warm the air feels against your skin. Can you hear your shoestrings snap, snap, snap? While our feet move across the ground, let's allow our story-writing challenges to float around in our minds like lazy clouds. In letting go of angst, new insights may spring up and out of the well inside us. Whether into the wilderness or onto our neighborhood sidewalks, get out and enjoy the movement of your breath, your feet, and your stories.

Prose about Walking Turns into Poetry

Don't be shy about recycling your writing, even from one form to another. Sometimes it can produce a surprisingly new piece. For instance, in 1987, I wrote a paragraph for a college English class assignment that asked us to incorporate all five senses. I filed that paragraph away, kept it all these years, and recently turned it into a poem. Below is the original paragraph titled "A Roadside Walk," followed by the poem "Arrangements."

A Roadside Walk

It lay in a long pile at the edge of the road, stretching out in front of me for about a hundred yards. Some blades were already turning pale yellow under the heat of the sun. As I went shuffling through it, the laces on my worn tennis shoes flopped rhythmically around with a snap, snap, click, click. To my left, the gray pavement lay hard and stony in contrast to this soft, green cushion under my feet. The newly mown pile offered me adventure. Kicking it up with each step, I delighted in the similar satisfaction I get from kicking up loose, fluffy snow and plowing through leaves piled high in a gutter. But the defenseless grass did not rustle as loudly as dried leaves; it sifted almost as quietly as snow around my feet after each kick. As it did, I caught a whiff of its sweet aroma. Pleased by the nearly featherweight green dancing up and down in the air and falling gently to the ground, I happily continued shuffling ahead until there was no more.

Arrangements

They form a long mound of tiny hay,
a refuge for crickets and fleas at the edge of the road.
I embark on disrupting their arrangement
for about a hundred yards.

They are pale now and dry,
soft yellow, shades of beige.
I shuffle, and in the shock of my disturbance
they dance.

They are restive and spill and scatter.
I stride through their feathery formation,
as if through a cover of crystal snow or
a gutter full of old surrendered leaves.

They shift—reorder around my intrusion—
sublime in nonresistance,
resettle   in   scattered   patterns,
send creatures running, rearranged.

📖 Reading I Recommend about Walking

The Sense of Wonder: Words and Pictures to Help You Keep Alive Your Child's Inborn Sense of Wonder, and Renew Your Own Delight in the Mysteries of Earth, Sea and Sky by conservationist Rachel Carson.

"Why Walking Helps Us Think" by Ferris Jabr. *The New Yorker.* September 3, 2014.

The Magic of Walking by Aaron Sussman & Ruth Goode. From the cover: "The most complete guide ever published to the joys of walking ~ for pleasure, for health, for serenity ~ in city, in country, in America and abroad. Plus a glorious ramble through the literature of walking."

"I will arise and go now," William Butler Yeats, from his poem "The Lake Isle of Innesfree."

So WHAT? Writing Here Alone Together

Whether you are a member of a writing critique group or not, consider having a WHAT group once in a while to augment your writing life. I came up with the acronym—Writing Here Alone Together—but the concept is not new. All it means is that I invite a group of writer friends over to my house to sit and write.

When I hold WHAT sessions, they always give me a nudge to keep writing. Here's how it all started (before the COVID pandemic hit; we're still on pause these days). Since I write in a journal nearly every morning by myself, I thought it might be fun to invite a few nearby writer friends to share my quiet time and space. So, I did, and I'm glad others liked the idea, too. About eight of us meet in my living room / dining area: that's the limit for my WHAT.

What We Do

To an outsider, we might look as though we are students in a library. We each choose a suitably distanced spot in my living room, front porch, or dining room, and we sit with our heads bowed over keyboards or pens and notebooks—I prefer to write by hand in my copybook/journal. After everyone settles in, I set a timer for one hour. ONE WHOLE HOUR. No one speaks or moves from their seat, except for bathroom breaks, until the timer dings.

Something Additional We Do (I hope!)

By making time for WHAT, we make a deliberate choice to leave behind familiarity and also any guilt at taking the time to write. This is important. Recently, a writer friend reminded me that once, very long ago, she complained to me about the many writing distractions she had from family. She said my reply has stuck with her: "No one will respect your writing time until you do." I'd forgotten I can be that blunt. Apologies if it sounds harsh, but isn't it the truth?

What We DON'T Do

This get-together may be more about what we don't do, than what we do. We don't speak for an hour. We don't read books. We don't text, email, or make phone calls. We don't read our work aloud to each other. We don't critique one another's work. We don't give out assignments. I don't set a date for our next meeting—it's not a regular event. We don't make excuses for why we didn't come last time or slush around in guilt about it. (I hope not!)

Timers Help

While I worked on my memoir, *Undertow*, I got into the habit of setting a timer for forty-five minutes per regular session. All I did was think, write, sit up straight, rewrite, and try to breathe evenly. Focus, focus, focus. When I heard the ding that signaled the end of my session, I got up from my chair, stretched, did a few shoulder rolls, and walked up and down the hallway outside my writing/guest room. For the WHAT group, though, I give us a full hour. It flies by.

Personal Accountability

In the WHAT hour, each of us practices what I view as answering to ourselves. In the end, writers must face the music (the writing) alone, anyway. That's how I see it. During WHAT, we are independent writer-bees simply buzzing in the same garden and good vibes, concentrating on our own material. Intense energy, imagination, and dedication, along with love, patience, and intentionality, thrive under this roof for that brief period. To me, it is a gift like no other.

At the End of the Hour

We come up for air like scuba divers rejoining life on the surface. As we resume talking, some speak in whispers, perhaps timid about breaking the silence, or wanting to hold on to it. Soon, we stand around in my kitchen, munch on bagels, drink coffee, and open up about whatever is on our minds. At these get-togethers, while others might chat about their writing, I usually prefer not to discuss the work I did that hour. Don't get me wrong. I'll definitely get feedback on it, but I'll do that another time. No one can talk me out of the need to get feedback from trusted, experienced writers. Their constructive criticism, suggestions for change, and insightful questions about the material get me to clarify what I'm trying to do in a piece of writing and push me to improve it. That's how I grow. That's fertilizer for every writer's work.

What Good Is This?

Writing with other writers offers support. We're in it together. We each have intimate knowledge of the joys and challenges of the process, and that creates a bond. We've just experienced a time of trusting the process, trusting ourselves to bring something new into the world, some work that brings more beauty into it. Some WHAT members have shared that being in a different space from their own home or office refreshes them, is a welcome change: they are not tempted to get up and do stuff, like put in the laundry or check email. My hope is that writing in an environment unlike the one we're used to creates new patterns in our brains, new neural pathways that prompt different ways to express ourselves and invigorate our work.

So WHAT? Try it. You might like it.

Is This Your Season to Keep Writing?

Santa Claus flies a sleigh pulled by reindeer, lumbers down brick chimneys, and stashes gifts under light-strewn evergreens. In operating rooms across the country, surgeons dress in hospital-green outfits, don paper masks, and remove tumors from unconscious patients. Behind closed doors, writers sit in desk chairs while they read, think, and write stories, novels, nonfiction books, children's books, memoirs, poems, and plays.

We hear, "You are what you do." How about, "Do what you are." Are you Santa? Are you a surgeon? Are you a writer? If you're a writer, wherever and whenever you approach a page, lay down words—one, and another, and another, and another. Write sentences whenever you can. Write them despite a busy holiday schedule. Write them *because of* a busy holiday schedule. We are writers. Writers create, writers compose, writers stick with it. We do that.

Writing Gifts

Here are a few gifts from Santa—oops, I mean other writers. These were gifts to me that I give to you with best wishes for your writing life.

May Sarton, in her book *Journal of a Solitude,* wrote:

> My own belief is that one regards oneself, if one is a serious writer, as an instrument for experiencing. Life—all of it— flows through this instrument and is distilled through it into

works of art. How one lives as a private person is intimately bound into the work.

Amy Tan, in her book *The Opposite of Fate: Memories of a Writing Life,* wrote:

> When you are told, "It was meant to be," ask, "Who meant it? What does it really mean?" Is someone trying to make you accept an undesirable situation or one in which you have doubts? When you are told, "Shit happens," remember that plenty of other things happen as well, such as generosity, forgiveness, ambiguity, and uncertainty. When you are told, "It's simply fate," ask yourself, "What is simple about it? What are the alternatives of fate? What is fate's opposite?"

Edmund Morris in his essay "On Becoming a Writer" in the anthology *The Writing Life: Writers on How They Think and Work,* edited by Marie Arana, wrote:

> I grew to love the silence, even the mini-silences that swelled between one word and the next, and to this day, when words won't come, I listen for them rather than look for them. Sooner or later one that sounds right will whisper itself onto the page.

Enjoy your writing holidays wherever they may fall on the calendar.

Experiment with Writing Prompts

Do you sometimes have trouble deciding what to write about? Consider using a prompt to jump-start the process. Remember the prompts our grade school English teachers foisted upon us in September and thereafter? "What I Did on My Summer Vacation," followed by holiday-themed essays for Valentine's lovey-dovey-ness, Halloween horrors, Oscar-nominating praises for Mother's Day, and December's glorious array of religious holidays? (I don't mean to neglect Father's Day, but that came *during* summer vacation.) While my original assignments are long gone, I recall some of those essays and cringe. But they have their homegrown value. If nothing else, for fodder in an essay like this. Also, it seems they can perform like "starter" does when you make chewy sourdough bread. Or to put it another way, prompts are jets that take flight from a narrow runway, then once airborne, we steer them in any direction we like. Here's an example.

A Runaway Turkey Writing Prompt
Brainstorm a memorable Thanksgiving for five or ten minutes. How? Scribble some notes about what you ate, who was there, what kind of weather affected the event. Let your imagination delve into an aspect of that special time, perhaps the food. Food is always fun—good or bad. Write a paragraph about the roasted turkey your favorite aunt cooked. It was golden brown, and you saw the steam rising from it after Auntie Caroline set it down on the dining room table. Add the part

about your hunger for Auntie's three-inch-thick pumpkin pie topped with mountains of homemade whipped cream. Colorfully describe your aunt as if she's a character in a novel: "Auntie Caroline had hair the same golden shade of brown as the pumpkin pies she baked."

When you're ready, look at the beginning of that paragraph about turkey and pie, and slice it off. Make your now-fictionalized aunt, whom you rename Marie, alive on the page. To do that, cherry-pick some of your real aunt's glorious and inglorious idiosyncrasies, e.g., "… whenever she chatted in the kitchen with her most unfavorite sister, Aunt Marie switched on the exhaust fan." Or place her in a different setting—perhaps alone at a corner table in El Floridita, one of Hemingway's favorite bars in Havana, Cuba. It's her sixtieth birthday. She's all alone. Go with that and see what happens—perhaps a conversation with Ernest?

Stories Born from Writing Prompts

Whatever prompt you employ to jump-start your writing session, make friends with it, continue freewriting about it for fifteen minutes, brainstorm different ideas surrounding it by looking at photographs or out the window. Ask yourself as many questions imaginable about the topic and then answer them in different ways. Savor this process as you do that scrumptious pumpkin pie. Like an experienced chef who no longer follows a formal recipe but instead trusts her instincts about how much cinnamon to use, you'll discover ways around, over, or without the original prompt to follow what's more interesting to you.

The goal is to shape the post-prompt sentences into a solid piece of work that stands on its own, just as sculptors describe what happens as they chisel away pieces from a block of stone to reveal the figure within.

* * *

Fun fact: The original forms of three short-short stories included in this guidebook in *Part X: More Melanie Stories*, arose from prompts: "Melanie's Sign," "Nocturnal Impositions," and "A Farmer Secret." The prompts, required to begin and to keep in the stories, came from

The Florida Writer magazine in its featured section "Paragraphs," for which stories are to be 700 words max. Here's the prompt that inspired "Melanie's Sign." In its original form, the title was "The Sign."

> Write about someone who stumbles upon an abandoned object that is oddly out of place. Perhaps a wedding ring is spotted dangling from a tree branch, or a stack of family photographs is found stuffed in a handbag for sale at a thrift store. Does the person recognize this item? Does he or she keep it or try to find the owner? Make the discovery an integral part of your piece.

I'm happy to say "The Sign" was published in *The Florida Writer* magazine, October 2015.

* * *

📖 Books I Recommend for Finding Writing Prompts

The Writer's Idea Book: How to Develop Great Ideas for Fiction, Nonfiction, Poetry and Screenplays by Jack Heffron. Includes more than 400 prompts.

The Writer's Block: 786 Ideas to Jump-Start Your Imagination by Jason Rekulak.

What's Your Writer-Context?

One fact about writing stories is that we populate them with characters in various contexts: on a rustic farm, in an overcrowded city, on a sailboat lost at sea. We put thought and time into shaping relevant scenes, but how often do we consider the flip side of our writing reality: the context in which we do it?

What's Your Writer-Context?
Surely the time of day, the people we live with, and our nation's societal/political environment affect our writing on some level or another, as do our writing spaces, e.g., writing at a desk, in a coffee shop, or on a bed. If your context is anything like mine, it may shift, even from hour to hour. It's full of inspirations and exasperations. It reflects underlying ideologies. The makeup of who we are, what we believe, and where we live often seeps through onto the pages and shapes what comes there like an invisible hand.

Long ago, one of my writing instructors pointed out that *all* writing, not solely memoir or autobiography, is autobiographical. Even fiction reveals bits of who you are, what you value, your level of education, your sense of humor (or lack thereof). You and your interior and exterior contexts show up in tone, sentence structure, and diction.

Thank You, Mr. Junod

The impact of the writer-context on our work struck me while reading the article "What Would Mister Rogers Do?" by journalist Tom Junod in the December 2019 issue of *The Atlantic* magazine. I'll tell you about the piece, but first, let me give you some context for *that*.

At the time of that article, a new movie was released about Mr. Rogers, *A Beautiful Day in the Neighborhood*, which I wholeheartedly recommend. (If you don't know, Mr. Rogers had a very successful television show for children that lasted many years.) The movie is based on Junod's 1998 story for *Esquire* magazine "Can You Say … Hero?" It describes his life-changing relationship with the famous Fred Rogers, known for his kindness. In the movie, Junod is renamed Lloyd Vogel, portrayed by actor Matthew Rhys. Here's the bit from *The Atlantic* that stopped me in my reading tracks:

> I had been thinking of starting this story at one of those points of departure [how Junod was affected by a lesson of Mr. Rogers'], at one of those beginnings or one of those endings. But stories don't only speak: they are spoken to, by the circumstances under which they are written. And so, I have to start by mentioning that I have begun writing a story about Mister Rogers the day after two young men armed with assault rifles killed a total of 31 people in El Paso, Texas, and Dayton, Ohio.

How's that for a writer-context for Junod constructing his intimate story about Mr. Rogers, a gentle soul who advocated for kindness, for raising children to be kind, the sort of children the "young men armed with assault rifles" evidently were not?

What Is Speaking to Your Stories?

I love Junod's remarkable sentence, "But stories don't only speak: they are spoken to, by the circumstances under which they are written." This seems so obvious that I hesitated to write about it; however, it's holding me like a vise, so I decided to take the sage writing advice I received a long time ago: write your obsession. Now that's a writerly context—consumed by an obsession.

After reading Junod's article, I often am more conscious about how my context affects what I'm writing; it hangs like an invisible backdrop, one that provides color, sound, ambience. On the backdrop is a mural of the country, state, town, and house I live in. It also includes the weather, the noises impinging on my nervous system (I prefer writing in silence), the pen or computer I use. As I write this, I stop more often to check up on myself. I wonder, "What is speaking to my work in this moment?"

For instance, Mary Ann Evans, known by her penname George Eliot (1819-1880), was one of the greatest Victorian novelists and she portrayed the harsh reality of life in rural England in her masterpiece *Middlemarch*. Each character's story offers something different about human nature and coping with conditions in England back then. Composing novels during Queen Victoria's reign in England was an overwhelmingly large part of Eliot's writer-context.

The overriding writer-context for me while composing this guidebook is the persistent COVID-19 pandemic, as in "it's everywhere." So far, a thundering public health crisis of this magnitude has occurred only once every one hundred years. Its incomprehensible (at least to me) in its catastrophic effects. It's invaded nearly every corner of every society in every country on the entire planet Earth. Tragically, as I write this on December 20, 2021, at 7:21 a.m., this virus and its variants has killed 5,356,387 people around the world.[9] I knew a few of those unfortunate people. I wish I could say it is possible to remove myself from this depressingly sad context (a monumental understatement), to not let it affect me, to not think about it at all, but I cannot.

In contrast, my writer-context also includes art, the relief joy brings as when I viewed a recent documentary film about a most creative

---

[9] COVID-19 Data Repository by the Center for Systems Science and Engineering (CSSE) at Johns Hopkins University, https://www.arcgis.com/apps/dashboards/bda7594740fd40299423467b48e9ecf6.

music group: *The Beatles: Get Back*.[10] During this film, viewers are brought into the room with this foursome as they develop in real-time many lyrics and music that we're long familiar with now. As a writer, it made me appreciate more the synchronicity of the creative process as I bore witness to theirs unfolding in front of me. No matter how many dark elements may fill our writer-context at any given time, may art continue to shine its healing light.

Multiple Writer-Contexts

Let's hear another voice on this subject of writer-contexts: poet and philosopher David Whyte. In his book *Consolations: The Solace, Nourishment and Underlying Meaning of Everyday Words*, he writes:

> Maturity is the ability to live fully and equally in multiple contexts, most especially the ability, despite our many griefs and losses, to courageously inhabit the past, the present and the future all at once.

As writers, don't we aim to develop multiple worlds of stories, often drawing from our own experiences that have taught us how to live fully in different contexts, or in spite of them? I suspect our ability to navigate varying circumstances (traveling is a great way to challenge that) helps us imagine how to depict our fictional characters responding to changing situations we invent for them.

---

[10] From Wikipedia: *The Beatles: Get Back* is a 2021 documentary series directed and produced by Peter Jackson. It covers the making of the Beatles' 1970 album *Let It Be*, which had the working title of *Get Back*, and draws from material originally captured for Michael Lindsay-Hogg's 1970 documentary of the album.

Velcro Moments—Making Your Writing Stick

A Velcro moment is a bit of writing that sticks with a reader. Velcro, you probably know, is a strip of fabric with tiny "hooks" that "mate" with another fabric strip that has smaller loops. These strips attach to each other until pulled apart. (Thank you, Wikipedia.) Isn't Velcro a perfect image to illustrate how readers get hooked on your writing because you hooked them?

How do we make our writing unforgettable? National Book Award winner Barry Lopez offered gems of advice about this in 2010 at the Rollins College "Winter with the Writers" Literary Festival. In addition to reading from his stunning award winner *Arctic Dreams,* this remarkable essayist, author, and short-story writer conducted a free master writing class. I attended and took copious notes that have stuck with me ever since. Keep reading. They may stick with you, too.

How Do We Create a Velcro Moment?

To make our writing stick, Lopez urged us to create intimacy with the reader. When we write memoir, for instance, we create intimacy with readers by making ourselves vulnerable. We need not be afraid to show we are imperfect, letting readers in on our weaknesses and secrets. People relate to imperfection; for certainly no one who reads your work is perfect. None of us are. Similarly, when we write fiction, we aim to create characters with flaws and failings—as if they are *real* people, well-rounded humans who are sympathetic *and* memorable—and show whether and how they overcome those imperfections.

Notes Stuck on a Mirror

What Lopez taught that day impressed me so much that I taped my Lopez notes to a dresser mirror in my writing/guest room. Each note reminds me of the importance of being stuck to creating moments made of Velcro.

These notes are not in order of importance. They just reflect the order of my writing them in my notebook while Lopez, scrawling on a whiteboard to illustrate paragraph-making, relayed his observations about notable writing.

1. The *Velcro Moment*. Create intimacy with the reader by making/showing yourself to be vulnerable.
2. When is the story done? When it sounds right, it is cohesive; it sticks to itself.
3. Novels—remind the reader of something they already know.
4. Poetry—its essence is not of the intellect; it is of feeling and it's physical.
5. Metaphor—an idea is being pursued and advanced. The net is the story. The live fish inside is the idea being advanced.
6. Ending a sentence with an open vowel tells you to keep going. A closed consonant, a hard sound, ends the paragraph.
7. Writing is music.
8. The paragraph is geometry. Fill in the middle ground between the first and last sentence. The adjective used at the beginning falls like stone through the paragraph, creates an environment, a feeling for the whole paragraph in the subconscious of the reader.

9. Really different kinds of adjectives should be used to describe a noun.
10. Use the senses—not just the five, but our sense of location, space. The sonic environment elevates the scene.
11. Proprioception—feel the presence of others. Serves as motivation for a character to move. Example: Hear the phone ring in the kitchen, so leave the living room and walk back to the small kitchen to pick up the receiver and listen to the voice on the phone say hello.
12. Bring the reader into the scene—this creates a "felt" experience. It puts the reader there with you, so they feel it, too. That way, the story isn't just about me, they are there with me in it, and so the story is about us, not me.
13. The back side, around the corner, off in the distance, behind the potted plant a small lizard rose up on its front feet, puffing out its orange pouch to show its dominance over the threat I posed him.
14. Who are we writing to? *The part of myself that I want to be.*
15. Write despite the fear; it never goes away.
16. We are patternmakers, that's why we write.
17. I want to get someone to enter the scene with me. I need to work with it until it has a 360-degree reality.
18. Senses take us to the front; memory takes us to the places around the back.
19. Orientation. Steer clear of the "security camera viewpoint" of a scene. Move us around in the scene.
20. Observations and memory. Shifts in verb tense.
21. Mention something not in view. Create the past behind the present.
22. Make room for the reader in the scene.

23. Avoid using "it" or "there is."
24. Create something beautiful that lifts up the reader, does not diminish others. No pointing fingers.

My favorite is #8: the paragraph is geometry. What's yours?

Nudge Reports: Making Impossible Dreams Come True

Do you yearn for a better way to organize your writing projects? Do you have a big one to manage, such as a novel or memoir? Does publishing your work seem like an impossible dream? Let me share a method that helped me. A few years ago, while I was writing my memoir, a friend told me about a little book, *The ONE Thing: The Surprisingly Simple Truth Behind Extraordinary Results* by Gary Keller with Jay Papasan. In the book's chapter ten, "The Focusing Question," we see this wise saying from Mark Twain, "The secret of getting ahead is getting started. The secret to getting started is breaking your complex overwhelming tasks into small manageable tasks and then starting on the first one."[11] Keller's book about how do to what Twain advised gave me a big push in the right direction, prompting me to focus on what my heart told me to do—write and publish.

The Importance of Being Earnest

I put my focus where my heart was by generating weekly progress reports. These reports tracked my to-do tasks related to the book. Thus, *Nudge Reports* were born. The name derives from a friend who'd called herself a good "nudge" because at every opportunity she asked me

---

[11] Thanks to QuoteInvestigator.com, I discovered that Mark Twain didn't actually say this, but they're wise words no matter the source! https://quoteinvestigator.com/2018/02/03/start/.

how my writing was going: was the book finished, did I have a publisher yet? After about six months of rejection slips, she said, "If you don't find a publisher soon, tell me you'll publish it yourself." She's a friend who is hard to argue with. I said, "I will."

Accountability

I could have typed up the *Nudge Reports* and kept them to myself, but I didn't. Instead, I took a step toward accountability—a concept from Keller's book. I asked another friend, a fellow writer, for help.

> Dear Friend,
> ... Since you are my most helpful critic who "gets" the writing life AND you care about me, would you be willing to just read a weekly report I'd send you regarding my writing progress and news of what stage I'm in as far as publishing the book?
>
> This plan is to give me a person I am responsible to regularly inform, which should give me a reason to push myself more. If I know I have to report to you on Friday night each week, then I'll be more organized in my planning ... I think. We'll see. On Fridays I go to yoga and get home about 7 pm. I'll send you an email [report] afterward. Anyhow, you don't have to do anything. Just let me email you on Friday nights. Hey, how hard can that be? Of course, if you have any ideas to share back with me, you know I'd love that. But NO PRESSURE on your part.

Nudge Report Content

My friend, thank goodness, agreed, and so I began. By that time, I'd worked on shaping a book for eight years. That extra step of making myself vulnerable to another person kept the fire burning hotter than it might have otherwise. The *Nudge Reports* came from daily task lists I'd handwritten on 5" x 7" notepads—yeah, I'm old-fashioned.

The lists simply detailed every task I wanted to finish each day.

After I completed a task, I checked it off. The ones I didn't do rolled forward to the next day's list, or an appropriate one after that.

A rule to remember: Learn to be realistic about how much you can do in a day; otherwise, discouragement nips at your keyboard—and your soul.

Structuring Nudge Reports

I divided *Nudge Reports* into sections to keep tasks organized. Since I wrote them in emails, it was easy to use the Search feature to find items of interest or review them to make sure I'd accomplished a task. Over time, these reports became a research library of the steps I took to create my book and complete related projects, such as my website, articles, blog posts, and networking contacts. The sections?

GOALS SET FOR THIS WEEK
I copied and pasted the tasks from the previous week's *Nudge Report* that appeared under the heading GOALS FOR NEXT WEEK. After each task, I typed DONE or NOT DONE.

A rule to remember: Reject reprimanding yourself about items NOT DONE. You may discover some are needless. Drop those off the list.

TASKS DONE THAT WERE NOT LISTED ON LAST WEEK'S REPORT
These were afterthoughts or unexpected things to do, such as revise a chapter in response to a first reader's comments.

READING
This section tracked books I read while I was writing my own book, like *The ONE Thing*.

GOALS FOR NEXT WEEK
Here, I copied NOT DONE items from the GOALS SET FOR THIS WEEK section and added new tasks.

Be Your Own Nudge

I admit that sometimes I emailed my *Nudge Reports* late, but I sent them anyway. Worth it? You bet! One year and one month later, I self-published my book. Is your heart telling you to finish a book? Try reading *The ONE Thing*, and find your *Nudge Report* friend.

The End: Are We There Yet?

Breaking up is hard to do, even with a story. It's even harder if you've written a book of any length. Have you ever watched a movie and two-thirds of the way through wondered how in the world they're going to end this story? Or read a novel and asked the same question? Let's face it: endings are hazardous terrain filled with landmines. Finishing with a flourish means we do our best to avoid unforeseen crevasses or loose gravel and lead readers into a final landscape where the story ends well. So, the question: what makes a story end well?

How to End ... Well
A few years ago, I read an invigorating anthology titled *The Writing Life: Writers on How They Think and Work*, edited and with an introduction by Marie Arana, author and former editor-in-chief of the *Washington Post's* literary section, "Book World." She included a super chapter by Muriel Spark, a novelist living in Italy, who says about endings:

> ... I have learned that happiness or unhappiness in endings is irrelevant. The main thing about a book is that it should end well, and perhaps it is not too much to say that a book's ending casts its voice, color, tone and shade over the whole work.

I love that. It leaves me with an image of a gigantic shade tree casting its protective shadows over a large, rambling house (the book). Although many readers seem to ache for happy wrap-ups, we writers need to remember that not all pieces of literature are destined to, need to, or should offer a feel-good ending. Don't we also crave useful insight into the human condition from an unexpected, disturbing ending done well? Keywords: *done well.*

To End Is to Do the Hard Thing
Endings are hard: hard to write and hard to bear if you love the story and want it to go on forever. I like heart-wrenching endings, thought-provoking endings, and even surprise endings if they compel me to reflect on either meaningful transformations that the characters have undergone, or the story's subtle twists and turns. What I don't like is an ending that annoys me with its trite or too-tidy finish. If the writer has led me well and prepared me, I want to be satisfied or more thoughtful at the end. How about you?

One of my favorite movies, *Casablanca*, starring sad-eyed Humphrey Bogart and the spectacular Ingrid Bergman, has a terrific ending that, in my view, really is the only possible one for that story. Jack Heffron, author of *The Writer's Idea Book: How to Develop Great Ideas for Fiction, Nonfiction, Poetry, & Screenplays*, says, "A good ending provides closure in which character, plot, theme, and tone match what precedes them in the story. If the star-crossed lovers in *Casablanca* had hightailed it across the tarmac, leaving Ilsa's husband behind, we would not be happy."

Now that's the truth, isn't it? If they'd run off together, the entire story would come across as false.

An Image at the End
A poet once told me this about endings: at the close of a poem or story, leave readers with an image. Images stick in our minds like Velcro, or at least have a better chance of remaining there than vague generalities. Rather than drawing out a laborious explanation to tie up the story, plant a suitable image that shimmers in the imagina-

tion—a burning bush, a violet crushed under the heel of a boot, or a strip of metal spikes embedded in the road. A picture might be worth a thousand words, but a well-written ending that incorporates an image is priceless.

From Hills Avenue

I know you better
now that you are gone.
I know you were scared at a time
you could not say it.
I know you wondered,
as I tossed in dreams
on the sheet by your side,
if I knew.

The kitchen stool,
stiff and silent by the door,
held me on a morning you did not.
"I dreamt you left me.
You're not thinking of it are you?"
I made that up.
You did not move.

Below my window,
Rain darkens the streets
that wore us out.
We don't walk now.
We sit in separate houses,
eat alone,
look at empty chairs.

IX

IT'S A BOOK, NOW WHAT?

Off the Cliff: From Manuscript to Printed Book

Writing a book is like jumping off a cliff. But fear not. As Ray Bradbury says, grow wings on the way down. For authors, a safe landing transforms a manuscript into a printed book. If you're adventurous, I'm here to tell you this: you can land your book by self-publishing. If you have the time, instead of paying an online "full-service book publisher," hire several freelancers. Through networking with other authors, you can find an experienced book structure editor, a book designer, a photographer, and a copy editor. If you can manage this arrangement, you may save a load of time, money, and aggravation. I did.

My guidebook was: *The Complete Guide to Self-Publishing* by Marilyn Ross & Sue Collier. It's well tested, with more than 100,000 copies sold. I also referenced *The Copyright Permission and Libel Handbook* by Lloyd J. Jassin and Steven C. Schechter and *The Writer's Legal Companion* by Brad Bunnin and Peter Beren. With these, I learned that self-publishing, although not easy, is possible.

Consider these steps:

1. Be sure you are ready to publish. When you are, edit again anyway. For guidance, I studied *Getting the Words Right, Second Edition: 39 Ways to Improve Your Writing* by Theodore A. Rees Cheney, *How to Write a Sentence: And How to Read One* by Stanley Fish, *The Scene Book: A Primer for the Fiction

Writer by Sandra Scofield, *Self-Editing for Fiction Writers* by Browne & King, *Writing the Memoir: From Truth to Art* by Judith Barrington, and *The Art of Subtext* by Charles Baxter. And many more.

2. Set a publication date and plan your tasks backward from that. My guide for this was *The ONE Thing: The Surprisingly Simple Truth Behind Extraordinary Results* by Gary Keller with Jay Papsan.

3. Hire a professional book editor. Every manuscript should be checked by a second set of eyes. When you interview editors, ask them for a sample edit of a few pages from your manuscript. An experienced editor can be especially helpful with the story's structure. The structure of a book is like the foundation, walls, ceilings, etc. of a house. It needs to have every part in the right place to ensure the house is a house that will stand.

4. Review your editor's recommendations. As the author, you make the final decisions.

5. Solicit feedback from a few readers.

6. When you are "finished" revising, on the last page type "END." That is good psychologically.

7. Hire a copy editor. This is a specialization. Many editors do not do copy editing. When interviewing, ask, "How many passes do you do?" meaning: How many times do they read the manuscript looking for corrections to make? If they don't understand the question, find someone else. Your copy editor should follow the style for your genre. For memoirs and fiction, it's usually *The Chicago Manual of Style* (CMOS). For journalism and business writing, it's usually *The Associated Press Stylebook*. Here's a good description about what copy editors do:

> Copy editors, also known as line editors and some-

times as content editors, usually look at everything from facts to grammar and formatting. These editors can do it all. Copy editors specifically study punctuation and grammar. They have extensive knowledge of the English language and are familiar with writing styles.[12]

8. Collect promotional blurbs from authors and experts. Provide complimentary copies of your manuscript and ask them to meet a deadline.

9. Hire a professional book designer. These artists make book interiors look like proper books, not fancied-up Word documents. Designers can make or break your book with the cover. Before hiring, evaluate samples.

10. Pay a professional photographer for an author photograph. Put it on the back cover or inside the book on its last page. Resist the temptation to use selfies.

11. Optional: form a Limited Liability Company (LLC) as your press. Mine is New Wings Press, LLC. There may be tax advantages.

12. Get your book printed and distributed. Check out print-on-demand companies. I chose IngramSpark. Why? Their free sample copy was high quality, they have many distribution channels, and their production process easily guides you through the steps to transform your manuscript into a beautiful book. You can call with questions, too. I love that.

Ready, set...jump!

📖 A Book I Recommend for Writers Seeking Publishers

The First Five Pages: A Writer's Guide to Staying Out of the Rejection Pile by Noah Lukeman

---

[12] https://www.bkacontent.com/12-types-of-editors-and-what-they-do/.

Mini-Marketing for Maxi-Messages

A writer aiming to self-publish her first book treated me to coffee recently to "pick my brain" about the marketing plan I used to promote my self-published book. I wasn't sure how much I could help her. No one-size-fits-all approach exists. Each book, depending on its genre and target audience and the author's relationships and reach, requires its own individual marketing plan, like a custom-tailored suit. My book, I reminded her, was a memoir. Hers was a cookbook. But for the pleasure of her company—and free coffee—I offered to clue her in about books, friends, and websites that help me. Besides suggesting she create an author's website (or hire a professional to do it), set up the About the Author feature for herself on Amazon, and add a book page on social media sites, etc., I also offered one simple approach for her to try right away.

What is it? Two 5½" x 8½" Flyers, or Seeing Double?

Create small flyers to carry your book's message. The purpose? To convey "fast facts at a glance" about you and your book. In a Word document, after you finish entering the information you want (suggestions below), print the page and cut it in half. Bingo. Double the pleasure, double the fun, i.e., ten pages gives you twenty fliers.

You may find a software program that designs something like this for you, but if you want to do it yourself, here are simple instructions.

Creating an Easy-Peasy Marketing Flyer for Your Book

1. Open a new Word document and on the Layout menu, select Orientation. Then select Landscape.

2. Again, on the Layout menu, select Columns. Select Two.

   Note: The goal is to create content in the left-hand column, then copy and paste it into the right-hand column. Voila, you have a page containing two copies of the same flyer. And the small size of the flyer makes it easy to fold and put in your purse, backpack, or computer bag, and distribute at book events.

3. This may seem obvious, but to begin, place your cursor in the top left corner of the page—in the left column—and insert a small photo of your book's cover, preferably in color, if you have a color printer.

4. Beside the photo, type your book's title and subtitle (if there's a subtitle) using font size 12. Bold it.

5. Below the title, but still to the right of the photo, add this information: your name, the book's genre, its cost, whether it's in paperback, hardback, and/or eBook, and where it is sold. Even include the ISBN number, if you want.

   Note: For the rest of the content, I use font size 11 so it all fits in the column.

6. Below that, list any award the book won, succinct quotes from reviews of your book, etc. Maximum: seven lines.

7. Below that, create three headings for the following sections and plug in the content. Consider the number of lines I suggest for each section. Perhaps use red font for these headings to make them stand out.

   a. What it's about: Summarize the story. Use part of your book description, which may be on the back cover of the book. Six lines.

    b. Why [book title] matters: Tell why it is unique. What about the story is different from any other? Is it nonfiction with content important to society? Eight lines.

    c. A taste of [book title]: Offer a short, poignant quote from the book. This is a free sample of your writing from the story you created. Show off! Three lines.

8. The last section is your author bio. To make your name stand out, put it in **UPPER CASE** and bold it. Six lines.

9. Select the book cover photo and all the text you just wrote.

10. Copy and paste the selected content into the column on the right. Save the document. Tweak content to fit in the columns.

Adapting This Template

Customize the template for *your* book's needs. Make it work for *you*. Be sure it reflects *your* good intentions. Don't fill it with marketing jargon that people hear all the time. The point is to spread the word about your wonderful book in a quick, easy-reference manner. Like a two-minute elevator pitch, only on paper.

Using Your Mini-Marketing Flyers

I tuck one of these flyers in the front of every book I sell in person. At book events, I have a stack on the book-signing table. You never know where these flyers might end up—hopefully not in the trash, but in the hands of another person besides the one who buys your book, like a friend at work, or a relative who may consider getting their own copy. Show your flyer to bookstore owners who offer to sell your book on consignment. Ask permission to place a stack of flyers on a shelf near your publication. That way, it's visible to browsing customers. And be sure you put a flyer inside each copy of your book on that shelf in the bookstore. Do it yourself. Get as creative with this process as you can.

    Never underestimate the power of a little flyer with a big message.

Marketing Flyer Example

To see the flyer I made for my book *Undertow*, refer to "Appendix 2 – Mini-Marketing Flyer" in this guidebook.

Additional guidance for marketing your self-published book is generously provided in *The Complete Guide to Self-Publishing: Everything You Need to Know to Write, Publish, Promote, and Sell Your Own Book* by Marilyn Ross and Sue Collier. Fifth Edition. It includes a chapter on social media marketing. I used this reference book to self-publish *Undertow* and the guidebook you hold in your hand.

X

MORE MELANIE STORIES

Let Father In

Melanie Craven was sixteen, and Father O'Connell knew it. Melanie's mother, Pearl, had recently invited him to their home for a special visit, and she needed Melanie to greet him. It was a Saturday afternoon when Father O'Connell arrived at the Cravens' front door. Predictably dressed in the black uniform of the church, he stood in the middle of the welcome mat and tapped the brass doorknocker several times, sending sharp *tap, tap, taps* ricocheting through the house.

When the taps came, Melanie was upstairs with Pearl in the bedroom Pearl used now, the one Melanie's sister had before she married and moved away. Pearl stood next to the bed, buttoning the housecoat she called a dress over her swollen abdomen. Her belly had become so big that, to Melanie, her mother looked pregnant—an impossibility by now. Melanie glanced down the front of her own dress, her stomach flat beneath the cotton print shift her mother helped her sew last summer. It was pale blue with large green leaves curled around bright orange and pink flowers. The pattern's cheerfulness had attracted Melanie to the fabric. To make the dress, they'd used Pearl's old Singer sewing machine, still in good condition. It sat covered with a towel on a worktable against the wall.

"Oh, my, Father's here already," exclaimed Pearl. "Hurry downstairs, honey, and let him in." She pushed her feet into her slippers and gave Melanie a pleading look.

"Yes, ma'am." Melanie felt cowed by her mother's slow, deliberate motions. Before she exited the room, she watched her mother ease herself down onto the edge of the bed and stay there. No one had to tell Melanie how sick her mother was, although no one had actually sat her down to explain the serious disease. She'd heard the name of it, but that meant little. What she witnessed meant everything: her mother's enlarged belly, her reluctance to go anywhere, even to Mass. Every week new lines appeared on her mother's face, tracing the on-going pain.

Melanie left the bedroom and ran downstairs, leaving her mother alone with scattered signs of lingering faith: her grandfather's crucifix on the old oak dresser, a cross made from blessed palm leaves stiffening in the corner of the mirror, a prayer book and rosaries—both black and worn—on the bedside table.

As Melanie opened the front door, stifling humidity rushed in along with Father O'Connell's churchy smell of incense and candle wax.

"Hello, Melanie. You look really nice today. How are you?"

Melanie noticed his black shoes, their gleaming tops like shiny bowling balls, small ones. She almost laughed.

She said she was fine, asked the priest in, and shut the door. Inside the house, Melanie thought he looked like a man out of context. And in fact, he *was* out of context, having never been there before. Melanie began sweating with discomfort at playing hostess to a priest.

"Mom's upstairs." She gave Father O'Connell a token smile, the one she used with grownups when she had to be polite. "We can go up there now."

He took off his hat and placed it on a nearby table. When they turned toward the stairs, Melanie noticed him brushing a stray white hair from the sleeve of his wrinkled black jacket.

Pearl had invited Father O'Connell, rather than another priest from the parish, because he acted overtly kind to her, and he had an influential connection with the archbishop of the diocese. She needed that right now.

Melanie started up the stairs, sad about this visit, thinking her mother dreamt too much about getting well. But she wasn't totally sure about that, and of course the family wanted Pearl to get cured. But so far none of the doctors' treatments had worked, and none of the prayers from anyone had made any difference, as far as Melanie could tell.

With each step Melanie climbed, her narrow dress, a straight shift with no side slits, pulled against her thighs. She heard Father O'Connell breathing behind her. On the wall of the stairwell hung pictures of wild birds in wooden frames her mother had positioned in a row at the same angle as the stairs. Whether Melanie went up or down, the birds stayed alongside her. Melanie's favorite: the one at the top of the stairs, the robin, its red breast puffed and proud.

In Melanie's recent dreams, she'd been flying like that robin throughout their neighborhood. She'd skim above the pink-blossomed dogwoods that lined the street and soar above pine trees, some taller than telephone poles. Ever since her mother had gotten sick, Melanie often wished to take flight ... to anywhere. But guilt weighed heavily on her heart. She knew she shouldn't wish it. Especially today. Father O'Connell, her mother had told her, was bringing something special that might strengthen her faith to be healed. Melanie wanted to be around to see that.

The priest and Melanie reached the first landing on the stairs. It was a small one. To the right was the door to her bedroom. She'd shut it before she'd run down to let Father in the house. To the left were three more stairs leading to a second small landing, and there they encountered Pearl leaning against the doorframe of her room.

"Oh, my dear Pearl, hello and God bless you," exclaimed the priest. He sounded slightly out of breath. "How do you feel today?"

Melanie's mother gave a weak sigh. "Welcome, Father. I'm all right. Thanks so much for coming over. Come on in here and sit down."

Melanie noticed her mother wince when she said that. She saw her put her hand against her lower back, too—either for support or comfort. Melanie had seen the gesture before and knew it might be for either reason. Her mother returned to the edge of the bed and motioned her priest friend to sit in the straight-backed chair opposite her. It was an old chair, the blue paint chipped and worn from extensive use. Melanie's sister had left it behind when she moved out.

"It's a real honor," began the priest as he squirmed into the narrow seat, "to bring the Lord's blessing to you." He looked around the room, nodding at the religious accoutrements. Melanie watched her mother, now settled on the bed, slide her hand into her housecoat pocket, pull out a wad of tissue, then dab a few tears away. Melanie remained on the landing.

"So sorry to cry like this," Pearl said. "I'm just so glad to receive your blessing, Father … I guess I'm overwhelmed." She smoothed her "salt-and-pepper hair" as she called it, and smiled at Father O'Connell. He glanced at the doorway, and from her spot out on the landing, Melanie gave him the smile again.

"My, my," Father nearly whispered. "Melanie is nearly all grown up." He nodded in her direction. "Come on over here, young lady, and let's take a look at you." He swept his hand through the air, motioning her into the room. Melanie only knew the priest from church. He'd officiated at her Confirmation ceremony two years earlier. And certainly, more than once, he'd heard her Confession and given her Communion. Melanie wanted to keep that churchy distance, but power like his was the ultimate power, no matter whose house he was in. She cringed at his personal interest and his command. To please her mother, however, she took a couple of steps into the room.

"Yes," said Pearl, "she's sure a young lady now."

Ever since she became a teenager, Melanie realized she'd have to get used to this "young lady" phrase of her mother's, a ridiculous reference if Melanie had ever heard one, but what made it extra disconcerting was how her mother applied it to so many different occasions and in various tones of voice: tender at times of soothing; scolding in times of reprimand; and in times, like this one, of admiration. This time, Pearl smiled when she used it, but if she thought the term brought Melanie any pride, she was wrong. It sowed only discomfort.

Her mother went on talking to Father O'Connell. "Why, it seems only yesterday she was just a little girl…" Looking at Melanie she added, "Honey, come on in here, dear, come over next to me and tell Father O'Connell how you made that beautiful dress you're wearing … sewing your own clothes, now doesn't that prove how grown up you really are, what a young lady you are?"

Melanie obeyed and murmured yes, she'd sewn the dress on her mother's portable Singer, but with a lot of help from her. The priest's eyes widened and his smile trembled as if he'd bitten into something sweet.

"My, my, such talent," he observed, "and it seems like you've developed a young lady's figure, too."

A what? Melanie stood stock still and silent next to her mother, staring first at the priest, then nervously glancing around the room, noting the prayer book, the curtains, the sewing machine before glaring down at the floor. She swallowed hard. Nobody said a thing.

Melanie expected her mother to show some surprise at her favorite priest's comment about her teenaged daughter, but she didn't. Not at all. To make sure, Melanie slowly took a step away from her mother to look directly at her face but saw only serenity, not the faintest shadow of disapproval.

Didn't Mom hear him?

No, it seemed as if she had not heard him at all, because just then Pearl reached over to Melanie and pulled the dress tight around her waist, making her budding figure appear more budding.

Tension rose like steam in the room. Pearl tilted her head from side to side, considering her daughter's waist and hips, as if trying to decide what angle looked best. Father O'Connell gazed at this in fascination, transfixed and jittery and tapping a heel against the floor. Melanie's thoughts scattered like mice in a thousand directions. *What's wrong with my mother? A priest is not supposed to think about "young ladies'" figures. Father should not be looking this way at me.* Clearly, he was looking.

"Excuse me, but I gotta finish my chores, Mom." She hoped her mother did not register the blatant lie, a most unoriginal excuse to escape the room, and headed for the door, all the while keeping her eyes lowered and away from her mother and the priest, her mouth shut in a thin, tight line.

"Oh my, well, see you later, young lady," Father called, leaning forward in his chair. "See you in church tomorrow."

Melanie couldn't get to her bedroom fast enough. Safe inside, her heart pounding, she left the door open an inch or two to eavesdrop on her mother and the priest.

"Too bad she had to rush off, but we should discuss why I'm here. So, look, Pearl, this is what I've brought you, a relic of Saint Lidwina, the patron saint of chronically ill people. She's known to ease the suffering and pain of many, many, many souls. The Archbishop of the Diocese himself—he and I go way back—dispatched someone who brought it to the parish house this week just for you…."

"Oh, my goodness. Look at that …"

"We usually don't take relics out of the church once we've acquired them, but I received special dispensation to bring it to you. You've got a great need, my dear Pearl, and I'm sure you've heard about the healing powers of Saint Lidwina, yes?"

"Of course."

"Good. Keep it here in your room all week if you like, and I'll come back for it next Saturday."

Melanie's Sign

Melanie Craven was about to climb the broken steps of the apartment building when she noticed something sparkle in the matted grass between the flooded street and the sidewalk. The object, only a few feet away, was impossible for her to identify. She leaned over and reached towards it. Her wet raincoat sagged, and grew heavy across her shoulders, but despite that and the thunderclouds and the car that splashed her in its wake, she swiped her fingers through the grass and scooped up the sparkle: a doorknob, a glass one, not cracked, not even chipped. But its metal attachment was gone, which left the glass piece without a way to be of use, like a light bulb missing its electrical cap.

How did this get lost? Melanie's imagination went to work. Maybe an angry girlfriend in the front apartment hurled it through the picture window. Perhaps it jiggled loose and fell as careless movers transported a broken door. She held it up. It twinkled like a galaxy in her palm, felt heavy as an apple. Its top was smooth, the underside rough where it once attached to its metal fitting. Melanie gripped it gently, the curved design fitting perfectly in her fist. Then it happened again. Mingled with the warm rain, bitter tears streamed down her face, so she stood there and let them fall, let the pain behind them pass.

She soon stopped weeping and slipped the glass treasure into her raincoat pocket. As she climbed the front steps, she noticed dandelions choked the adjacent lawn. The parking lot beyond was covered in uneven dirt, not gravel, and pale-green weeds lay flattened from tires.

The tailgate of a truck parked under a sprawling tree was rusty and full of dents.

Melanie, eager to be on time, shrugged off these discouraging signs and opened the building's door, nearly colliding with an unshaven man talking with a woman in the hall. She held a closed umbrella that had trailed rainwater all over the floor. Looking Melanie up and down, she frowned and walked off.

The man turned to Melanie. "Hey, I'm Rupert. You?" She'd barely spoken her name when he nodded and motioned with a sinewy arm to follow him up the stairs. Every other one creaked. The color of the stairway carpet—worn through in the middle—reminded her of the darkest of walnut shells. Over his shoulder, Rupert mumbled, "Too bad about the storm. Have a hard time gettin' here?"

"Oh no, I don't live that far. Saw the rental sign in the yard this morning and called you." Melanie shed her raincoat as she clambered along. When they reached the top of the stairs, she held her raincoat against her, with the pocket that concealed the glass doorknob close to her body. "I really need to move someplace this weekend. My boyfriend just broke up with me."

"Oh, too bad, Miss." Without looking at her, Rupert rushed her down the hallway past a few doors, the overhead lights too dim to reveal much detail besides one burned-out bulb. The few ceiling fans were in the off position, useless in dispersing the oppressive humidity. Over his shoulder again, Rupert spoke, rattling off a summary of the building's "history," as he called it.

The Sunrise View Apartments were constructed during the 1920s in the historic part of town. Melanie was fully aware of this. She'd seen many houses in the district that displayed ornate bronze plaques with the proud proclamation "Historic Preservation Society." She knew this building lacked that designation. Its red brick exterior was solid enough, but window frames needed a paint job, and the interior was not up to any preservation standards she knew of.

On the two floors, there were ten small apartments—five up, five down—and, as she soon discovered, at least one needed repairs and deep cleaning. At the back of the building downstairs, she'd later encounter the junky laundry room scattered with lint and trash.

Rupert stopped his history speech to say, "This here's the one that's empty."

Melanie caught a whiff of his breath. It stank of onions.

"Just a sec." He fiddled with the doorknob, stuck a key in the deadbolt slot right above it and pushed the door open.

Within ten minutes, Melanie said she'd take it. Desperate times call for depressing apartments: one tiny bedroom, but big enough for her futon, chest of drawers, and antique desk. The kitchenette and living room (if you could call it that) were merged into one. The bathroom was strange but typical 1920s: a bathtub in a closet by itself, and next to that, in another closet, a sink and toilet. The two matching closet doors, like twins, were set into the wall of what Rupert called the living room. Melanie noted the crooked air conditioning unit, the unwashed windows, and the old glass knobs on the few doors. She smiled, thinking of the one she just rescued from the grass.

"I can go home right now, write a deposit check, and bring it to your office downtown in half an hour."

"Deal." Her new landlord raked one hand through his stringy hair and shook her hand with the other. She followed him down the soggy narrow stairs and outside, where they parted ways in the rain. He climbed into the rusty truck and drove off. Melanie, back in her raincoat, walked the few blocks to her current apartment building and trudged up those stairs to the third floor. Her newly-former boyfriend slouched in his Adirondack chair on their apartment's screened-in porch, staring down into the flooding street.

"What happened?" he called into the open doorway, setting his beer bottle down. "Did you like it? Can't believe you went there. He's such a slumlord. Everybody knows that. Geez."

Inside by her desk, Melanie pulled the glass knob from her raincoat pocket and set it like a crown atop her notes and papers. "Yeah, well, I'm moving in there," she yelled. "Got a one-bedroom. I've had a sign. A clear one." Eyeing her new treasure, Melanie wrote the check.

Nocturnal Impositions

Melanie Craven, snug in her cot, squinted through the lamplight half-reading her book, half re-examining her zigzag life, when she heard a tap against the tent pole. Had someone knocked on the pole as if it were a door? In the faded khaki light, she could not connect the sound with any shadow. The pattern of self-reflection—was her life formed more by what she'd done than what she'd failed to do?—spun through her thoughts as she considered the noise. Had a skittering creature tapped the pole and run?

She'd signed on for this tour to escape her techie career, think of new options. Down went her book on the blanket that Bob's Iberian Adventure Tours had provided; up struggled Melanie from the droopy cot. She loosened the cord of the tent's front flap, a demarcation between in and out, and let the canvas door fall open. Shocking, cold air covered her face. *No one.* She peered through the haze. She saw no moving figure, detected no human scent, heard no swish in the underbrush. Her movement toward the flap had been too slow. Melanie imagined the knock was just that: imagined.

In the morning light at the campfire breakfast, Melanie examined familiar faces. The hiker from California with tanned rivulets mapped on his face sat cross-legged on the ground. He scraped his fork across the surface of the gunmetal plate to rescue every scrap. The iron skillet, steady on a flat rock, held more overcooked eggs, as well as the hiker's attention. Close to the fire ring, the honeymooners from San Salvador whispered their secret language while perched next to each other on one large rock. Melanie felt a pang of envy at their sweet commiseration. Both scientists, they specialized in the study of bats. Melanie wondered whether such work had drawn them together, night after night, but might someday drive them apart. On separate boulders worn smooth from years of travelers' bottoms, sat Mrs. Devona and her husband. He had not yet spoken this morning, not that Melanie had heard, but she did hear Mrs. Devona, a spike of a woman, prattle to the guide.

"Why in heaven's name is it so cold here in the jungle at night? That brook behind our tent is freezing, as cold as the Arctic Ocean. And I thought this was supposed to be spring."

In the fire pit, ashen embers, orange embers, crackled and fell apart.

Melanie waited as the guide—fortysomething, totally gray—thought of a reply to this woman. He gazed up at the pale morning sky and said, "But isn't the air invigorating here? No pollution!" No one responded. He took a quick gulp of coffee from his metal cup then said, "And the green trees and grass all around! It's just awesome!" He raised his cup in a salute, adding, "And don't you all just love the variety of songbirds here? Absolutely amazing!" In that moment, coffee sloshed out of the cup and landed on his shirt sleeve, but he didn't flinch. From the front pocket of his travel vest, the kind Melanie saw in catalogs, he pulled out the familiar red kerchief dotted with stains and wiped his shirt and forehead with it. When she'd first met this guide, she'd wondered how he managed to move so easily inside the train, the bus, the jeep, given those bulging interior pockets. She'd nearly bought such a vest herself, but left that fashion mistake unmade.

What the guide claimed as amazing really was amazing, except Melanie believed silence was also amazing. If only the guide included that in his selling points for Mrs. Devona. But Mrs. Devona seemed the kind of woman unused to silence. She often referred to girlfriends back home and cocktail luncheons she missed because of this trip. Taller than Mr. Devona, she stooped to meet his eye. Today, she wore a candy-cotton pink scarf around her ropey neck. The Devonas hailed from Colorado. Melanie learned that from their nametags at the informal, get-acquainted, torturous mixer. Mr. Devona had just quit his executive job at a lumber company; outdoorsy experiences were his current penance. Melanie learned that while sitting in her assigned seat next to Mrs. Devona at the dress-up, superfluous, kick-off dinner.

After breakfast was abandoned, tedious repacking completed, and weather complaints efficiently side-stepped, they piled into the jeep. Melanie reclaimed her seat in the rear, her back to the group. From this position, she saw where they'd been, witnessed tire tracks grow in the dirt, became hypnotized away from the others, their gear, their talk … except for Mr. Devona. He had not yet spoken.

Mr. Devona, hunched beside his wife while gazing out at disappearing scenery, brooded over the flicker of khaki light, the canvas door, his trembling hand.

B Is for Baby Names

The last time Melanie Craven's aunt, Eleanor Moore, got pregnant, she wrote Melanie an email with the news and a plea:

Please, Mel, send me some names for this one. Boy names and girl names, okay? You're so creative. I just know you can help us. I'm stumped.

At names' end,
Auntie E.

Eleanor and her husband, Steve, already had eight kids, and conjuring up unique names had become a confounding issue. Their birth-announcement message delighted Melanie, but she had to admit that the medium for it did not. Melanie hated email. All day at her tech job, she opened, read, answered, sent, printed, deleted, filed, and sometimes ignored email communications from colleagues and clients. At home, in her private life, she rebelled.

For a few days Melanie mulled over various mainstream names, then quirky and even unheard-of names before she answered Auntie E. She ruminated on names during her morning power walks and glanced through a few books on sale about baby names. That gave her hours of fanciful pleasure. She was pleased to act as the creative person her aunt, so sweetly, believed her to be.

But she didn't answer the email. From a desk drawer, she pulled out a box of creamy white stationery—her best medium for such an honored task—and sighed over the lovely woven paper with matching envelopes. She'd bought it from The Paper Stash, a quaint and homey bookstore around the corner from work. That's where she'd skimmed the book of baby names. Over the last few years, after long days in her sterile cubicle, that shop had become her entertaining refuge.

Melanie cleared off her desk (an antique from Grandma), took a couple of sheets of writing paper from the box, and picked up her favorite fountain pen.

Dear Auntie Eleanor,

First, I'm thrilled you and Steve are bringing another little Moore into the family. What joy, especially during these days fraught with unprecedented national unrest, not to mention devastating economic stress, and this tragic COVID pandemic upending our lives. At the very least we're grocery shopping at ungodly hours to avoid picking up that wicked virus and bringing it home with the grapes.

Now, onward to the names. For the past few days during my morning walks through the neighborhood (can't really go anywhere else) and always wearing a surgical mask–imagine me with that thing on, but alas, it really is the common-sense thing to do–I thought over your naming dilemma. For hours I walked, circling my block of apartment buildings over and over, running down the alphabet in my mind to prompt possible names beginning with each letter for your newest baby. I didn't get through the entire alphabet with a list; twenty-six names might drive all of us mad. But ... I tried to find ones that might fit well with your last name: Moore. This was difficult.

The names I came up with may sound a bit old-fashioned or even strange, but without worrying over that too much, maybe one will stick.

It's possible you can use each name for either a boy or a girl, but who can be sure these days? So, take your pick. If you decide not to use any of them, I won't feel bad. This is YOUR baby, after all. Anyway, old Willy S. used to say, "What's in a name? That which we call a rose by any other name would smell as sweet."

Thanks again for asking me to chime in with my bright ideas, listed below.

Love and congratulations,

Melanie

Names best pronounced aloud with your last name, Moore.

Ahphew
Alotte
Dreenk
Ehver
Adding
Lilbit
Noah
Somme
Taek

A Farmer Secret

The last time Melanie Craven returned to Gladville, her hometown, was twenty years ago. She'd roamed the old neighborhood, explored Main Street, and visited familiar fields of sweet corn, their golden tassels blazing in the sun. This time, she'd include a visit with her mother's best friend, Louise Farmer, one of the few people Melanie still knew in Gladville.

According to letters Melanie received from Louise, she learned that Louise's grown sons, Mark and Alan, had moved away, married, and had kids. No surprise. As teenagers, they'd yearned to leave town. Melanie, single and teaching college a few states away, sometimes imagined moving back. She had no apparent reason for that, just a sense that something vital, something true, was there.

The train hissed into Gladville Station, and Melanie became eager, like a tourist. While she waited outside the station for Louise, the aroma of rich soil drifted by, soil that grew dark green soybeans almost instantly. Around the street corner came a faded blue truck heaped with vegetables. Behind it, children on bicycles shouted along the dusty road. Church bells rang the hour. Why had Melanie waited so long for this?

When she was little, the Farmer family lived next door. The kids went to school together until both families left the neighborhood for better homes on opposite sides of town. Melanie had missed those boys she considered brothers. Growing up, they'd all played, cried, and laughed alongside each other, not consciously registering their development. That is, until Alan, the cuter, younger son (Melanie's age) sprouted like a wild stalk of corn, his gangly arms and legs often outgrowing his clothes.

Years after, Melanie had boyfriends from high school on her side of town. She saw the Farmer family on Sundays, birthdays, and holidays, sort of like visiting relatives. Sometimes low-level attraction flashed between Melanie and Alan, but familiarity and awkwardness extinguished it. Now, before this trip, a few times in her sleep, Melanie had romantic dreams about gangly Alan. Waking, she dismissed them as residual energies from youth.

When the two long-separated women met, they hugged and hugged. Later, in the country silence of Louise's home, they caught up on life as much as people can in only an hour after years apart. Then Louise drove them to dinner. "My treat, dear," she said.

In the car, Melanie calculated how old her mother's best friend must be ... Louise's wrinkled hands were steady on the wheel, her sight quickly assessed the road, and her mind retrieved memories with clarity as she drove the car, so, whatever her age, Louise was still chugging along. Their conversation was a stream of comforting reminiscence of the two families sharing picnics at the city park and Easter egg hunts in the spring.

"We didn't have two nickels to rub together, back then," Louise said, "but we all sure were happy. Then your parents moved you guys out by the college, and we moved way over here. I missed your mother all the time."

"But we still visited a lot," Melanie insisted, trying to lighten the mood. "Sunday after church. And birthday dinners. Your cinnamon cake was divine."

Louise smiled and glanced in the rearview mirror as she drove toward the restaurant.

"And something funny I'll never forget," Melanie said, "at the last minute, Mom asked you whether or not one of the boys could take me to the prom because my boyfriend suddenly couldn't. He'd caught mononucleosis. Remember?" Louise let out a good laugh as Melanie continued, "Lord, was I devastated! This was THE PROM, the most important date of my life. I'd already bought a gorgeous yellow dress and booked a hair appointment. All down the drain. Then, out of the blue, Mom announced Mark would take me."

"Sure, I remember … but you know Mark really was not actually supposed to take you, right?"

"Huh?"

"It's true. Alan wanted to. But he waited 'til the eleventh hour to rent a tuxedo. When he rushed home and put on the jacket, the sleeves were too short. On Mark, they were perfect."

"Good heavens … no one ever told me." Memories of the strange prom night (as if a date with your brother), of Alan's lanky arms casting her fate, and of that pale, sick boyfriend long lost, tumbled through Melanie's mind, creating a dizzying swirl of emotions.

"Oh, honey," Louise chuckled, "isn't that something?"

XI

IF YOU WANT TO KEEP WRITING

A Writer's D-List

During one of my morning walks, just after the sun rose over leafy oak trees in my neighborhood, I found myself thinking (for the millionth time!) about why I write. What makes me want to? Why does anyone write stories, books, plays, and poems or anything that takes so much time, concentration, and angst? Why do we stick with it? What makes us push on?

The marvelous book *MFA in a Box: A Why to Write Book* by John Rember revives my heart when these questions loom. Rember calls me back to myself, to the part of my soul trying to make sense of my experiences, to make meaning of it all. He generously offers, "This book will give you solace in those dark nights of the soul, and it will give evidence that the sun eventually breaks the darkest horizon."

The following D-List is my shorthand way of offering comfort and bite-size encouragements to continue the writing life.

"D" Doesn't Always Stand for Near-Failure

Remember how the letter "D" on a test returned from your teacher meant far less than stellar work? Well, forget that. I'm here to tell you that many good qualities a person needs to keep writing happen to begin with the letter "D" used in a good way. These qualities, these ideas came to me during that morning walk in answer to those questions mentioned above. I see them as traits essential for a flourishing writing life. Funny (maybe coincidentally?) they all began with "D." I believe they can drive (another D) our writing like a powerful motor under the hood, propelling us forward. Let's keep the following list by our side to rev up our creativity. I include it here to close out this guidebook for the writing life. Each item has helped me get from the porch to the page. I wish the same for you.

Note: These "D" items are not in order of importance. For sure, we'll shuffle them around over the course of our lives.

Desire

First, when you want to write something other than a grocery list, ask yourself how much desire you bring to this idea or project. Do you love the core idea, or are you ho-hum about it? Are you passionate about writing this story, this novel, or this particular poem or self-help book? If not, do you think or hope your attitude will change if you proceed? It might. Go for a walk and see what happens, what your gut or heart tell you.

If you are wishy-washy about the project—or worse, down-in-the-dumps—why bother? Skip it, at least for now. If your heart is not in it, your negativity may cast shadows over the writing. You may even sabotage the work. Put it in the drawer, out of sight for a time. But never throw out any writing. Many stories come later from recycled work.

Desire, on the other hand, is a really-want-to sensation. It's a flame, small at first, that leaps into a raging fire as you feed it the fuel it needs. It pulls you toward the page, to get the sentences down, the descriptions clarified. Desire's positive yearning moves you along. It compels you, from deep down in your bones, to write the story only you can write, e.g., the one about the drowning Persian cat whose friend, a St. Bernard dog, drags it out of the fast-moving river and lays it gently on the nearby shore. Like the dog, who, out of love, selflessly dives into the freezing water to save his kitty-cat friend, you desire to plunge in and save the story from going under, to capture it, to bring it safely to the page.

Divert Unrelated Work

Tuck away in a folder those random ideas, colorful descriptions of cats, offbeat characters, cranky sounds, striking images of crying women, bits of overheard conversation on the train, shocking or subtle news stories of floods or murders, vexing ethical dilemmas, jumbled airline schedules, Christmas cookie recipes, wrong number phone calls, local train wrecks, kindnesses from strangers, and all the bits and pieces and flotsam and jetsam we scribble on torn napkins, paper towels, sticky notes, backs of envelopes, bookmarkers, margins of books we're reading, useless business cards, and expired coupons—anything we can grab at the moment something captures our attention, anything that pops up in a synchronistic way. Some of those captured items may not fit into our current work, so put them in a box or desk drawer. Don't lose them. Maybe on a rainy afternoon, sort through those scraps and categorize them, then type whatever they have to say into one or several Word documents. Consider these your grab bag of ideas, a reservoir to dip into, a charging station to spark your imagination, a supply of writing prompts. This way, you're not losing or discarding them, just diverting these potential gems from the work at hand, delegating them to another job, another story, another poem or song. Reuse, revise, recycle all your brilliant ideas.

Delete Distractions

For the sake of focusing on your work, ask yourself, "What am I willing to sacrifice?" To fully enter a different reality from outward daily life—an inward reality made of sentences, feelings, images—writers must temporarily disengage from the ongoing-ness of the world. Does this take effort? You bet! Herculean effort, sometimes. Oh, for a "Delete" key to do away with distractions. For the good of your work, you may have to miss the popular movie, the latest webinar, the happy-hour Zoom call with friends. Or maybe not. Let's say you can arrange your sessions of disengagement-with-the-world by creating a realistic schedule and closing the door—often literally. Other times, watch out. Your work-in-progress may gain the upper hand and insist you scrap the schedule (like a needy child you cannot ignore) and get to the page right now.

Determination

Determination is entwined with deleting distractions. Your determination to write the story within or even despite your circumstances, especially during difficult times like a global pandemic, will propel you to eliminate distractions. Breathe. Stretch. Open your heart to your imagination. Stay on task and bring to life the story you desire to write. Watch how a budding flower does this. It sticks with nature's program, slowly opening in its own time until the flower, its origins once hidden within the seed, finally blooms and creates more beauty in the world.

Tell yourself you will create one sentence after another to carry the drama, to describe the river, to portray lively details of the dog and cat in the water wrestling in their near-death experience. The story matters to you. Make it matter to readers. Keep writing against the stream of doubts from your inner critic or from people who inadvertently (or on purpose) demean your attempts out of jealousy, or from underestimating your ability (or other reasons). Prove them wrong. Get your gumption up and go. Consider this from Andre Dubus II, "But the writer who endures and keeps working will finally know that writing the book was something hard and glorious...."

Discipline

Discipline is a close cousin of determination. Exercising discipline—in body and mind—makes it possible for you to finish the work. You sit and write. You go for a morning walk or swim at the gym (that's what I do) and the work continues in your mind. A new idea emerges. With each step, your thoughts are on the scene of the river: you see the cat flailing in dark, icy water, and the dog paddling to save her. Later, in the kitchen as you make dinner, you imagine how to simplify the text, add a detail: the dog drags himself over a fallen log in the river. While brushing your teeth, you meditate on the story, consider new metaphors. This extra layer of ongoing-ness in your mind, invisible to others, is typical for a disciplined writer who loves the work.

I keep a copy J. Ruth Gendler's *The Book of Qualities* in my writing room for easy reference. Here's a gem she offers about the quality of discipline:

> Discipline does not disappear forever, but she does take vacations from time to time. By nature she is a conservative person, and yet she lives a radical life. Guided by a sense of inner necessity, she works hard and takes many risks. When Discipline was a teenager too poor to afford dance classes, she skipped lunch to pay for her lessons.

Delight in the Process

By including delight, I want to offset any scowling or scolding that sometimes accompanies conversations about discipline. Remember, we writers are foremost human beings (contrary to what some critics might say), and as humans, writers have sensitive feelings like everyone else, maybe more so. That sensitivity is key to our work, and it needs to flourish and not be squashed by old-fashioned ideas about discipline that bog us down or make us uptight, especially when we see lists of "you should-do-this and must-think-this-way." In the end, no one can tell you how to be disciplined as a writer because each of us is so very different from the next writer who comes along. My intention is to coax out and nurture a featherweight delight in our writing process. Savor moments when you get an interesting idea straight from the center of your soul. Trust that more will come. Smile at a funny sentence you write. Whenever you can, engender a playful, curious attitude toward the work, perhaps similar to how you felt as a child when you made Valentine cards from red construction paper and glued sparkling silver hearts on them. Laugh out loud at your bravery as you try something new or break a conventional writing rule in the name of creativity. Stay light.

A wonderful synonym for delight is *glee*. When we're gleeful, I imagine us rubbing our hands together in anticipation of more joy. Writing is a subversive act, some say, so celebrate that reputation. Feel the tingle of elation run up and down your spine. Grin in the mirror when you say, yes, yes, count me in. I shall go on creating. I will keep on writing.

Disregard Doubt

In her book *Me: A Memoir*, Brenda Ueland musters up choice words against the ill effects of doubt which undermine discipline and desire and delight, much like undertow pulls shells and seaweed out into the deep. In place of doubt, joy must live, Ueland says. I'll let her tell you about it in her own words as she describes how her friend, Francesca, a music teacher, helped her confidence with writing grow:

> ... what Francesca did for me: she began to show me that doubt, tension, grim resolution, are no good. It merely steels one into rigidity, and usually in defense against a pain or a difficulty, or an enemy that does not exist. She made me feel that life, gift, greatness is in all creatures, even animals, and that if we saw it and believed in it and generously loved and admired it and praised it in them, it grew. Yes, that is why we like praise: it is just a corroboration of what we are trying to do, and a sign that perhaps we are succeeding, so we can take heart and go on.

Sometimes "take heart and go on" means you must reject doubt and bad advice from other people that reveals their uncertainty about your writing ability, their underestimation of your capacity to know what's best for your story. No matter how well intentioned a friend's feedback on your work may be, even the kindest and most experienced writer friend, remember you still make the final decisions. You are responsible for what you write. Trust your gut, trust your intuition, trust your understanding of what the story needs. For instance, in *Undertow*, someone suggested I begin the book with a different first chapter than the one I had placed in that critical position. Although the suggested chapter contained a shocking scene, an attention-getter if ever there was one (hint: the cult leader catches us off guard by running a porno film during a Bible class), I rejected the idea of using it as the first chapter. Why? Well, I didn't want to throw that offensiveness in any reader's face right off the bat. I felt readers first needed time to adjust to the cult world I showed them before revealing the complex psychological drama of such a scene. But also, I disregarded that suggestion because the memoir is primarily about *my* journey of transformation, not about the abusive cult leader. He is not the main character, I am. What you read in the first chapter focuses the spotlight on me during a tenuous time, but on the road to escape.[13]

Dreaming, Sleeping, and the Imagination
While our bodies are fast asleep, our conscious minds get needed rest and our unconscious minds go to work. (Although simplistic, this description is useful for a short essay.) We call that sleeping work *dreams*. Consider your unconscious dreaming state as a dependable writing buddy. It scans deep dark issues that bother us, solves problems, conjures up solutions. Creativity's energies take center stage in our dreams, helping us make connections and plant new ideas through imagery. In her book *The Artist's Way: A Spiritual Path to Higher Creativity*, Julia Cameron reminds us we have our own unique creative self to express. I think our inner selves need high-quality sleep as much as our outer body-selves.

If we sleep well enough, we'll have a freshly rested brain/mind as our writing companion. (Regarding brain/mind: I suggest this educational project: investigate what *brain* and *mind* each refer to, how we distinguish their meanings.) As for tapping into ideas brought to you while sleeping, try this experiment: as soon as you can upon awakening, take a few breaths and jot down whatever comes to your now-conscious (or half-conscious) mind in the dawn of a new day. During that post-sleep phase, our inner creative self that we carry around all the time may hand us the lynchpin idea for our writing project. Perhaps

---

[13] You can read the first chapter of *Undertow* for free on my website: https://charleneedge.com.

this phenomenon is what we call a gift from The Muse. I'm not guaranteeing this will happen, but I have experienced it more than once. We've all heard the sage advice: set aside your writing project for a few days and just sleep on it. Literally, sleep is a restorative gift. Remember that. Whenever you feel frustrated or defeated, give yourself a break—a sleeping break. It's likely you'll see your work with refreshed eyes and seek out fresh words.

P.S. Don't forget: dreams and imagination are kissing-cousins. Robert Johnson, a Jungian analyst and bestselling author of many books, including *Owning Your Own Shadow*, delves into many aspects of the imagination in his book *Inner Work: Using Dreams and Active Imagination for Personal Growth*. Here's a paragraph showing his perspective on the topic:

> We may picture two conduits that run from the unconscious to the conscious mind. The first conduit is the faculty of dreaming; the second is the faculty of imagination. Dreaming and imagination have one special quality in common: their power to convert the invisible forms of the unconscious into images that are perceptible to the conscious mind. This is why we sometimes feel as though dreaming is the imagination at work during sleep and the imagination is the dream world flowing through us while we are awake.

Dreaming and Daring

When I was a young girl, my mother gave me a book of children's stories and poems called *Dreaming and Daring*. I kept that book with my others, including Grimms' Fairy Tales, several volumes of Nancy Drew stories, and probably a Webster's dictionary, in a small bookcase in my bedroom. I'd watch over those books like babies, settled in next to each other on the shelves, their black or green or dark red titles decorating their spines, comforting me, as if they were merry faces of friends.

On a page inside *Dreaming and Daring* was a line drawing of what looked to be a Viking ship perched atop rolling waves. It bulged like a filled-up Santa's pouch. Its tall sails resembled puffy clouds in the wind. That image fed an adventurous spirit in me, an audacious one, and I imagined launching off as a stowaway hiding below deck on a journey to far-off lands.

Today, I have forgotten the stories between the covers of that book, but its catchy title and the sketch of that ship have stayed with me. Over the years, if they had been voices, they would have been shouting, "Be brave. Don't give up!" I hope you hear them urging you to do the same. Together, let's dream and dare—and dare to write whatever we dream.[14]

---

[14] I recently found a copy of *Dreaming and Daring* through a used bookseller. It's a bit tattered, but oh, what joy! The content was compiled by Elizabeth H. Bennett, Mabel B. Dowse, and Mary D. Edmond and illustrated by Marguerite Klinke Scott. Published by Silver Burdett Company. 1953.

Appendix 1

TIMELINE FOR WRITING & SELF-PUBLISHING *UNDERTOW*

The following shows what turned out to be the timeline for writing and self-publishing my memoir *Undertow: My Escape from the Fundamentalism and Cult Control of The Way International*. New Wings Press, LLC. 2017. I did not plan this schedule ahead of time. It developed.

In this chart, you'll see mention of *Undertow's* brilliant copy/line editor, Ruth Mullen, to whom I lovingly dedicate *From the Porch to the Page*. Ruth died tragically in September 2021, just before we would have worked together again. She was a kind, wise, and go-the-extra-mile colleague.

Appendix 1: Timeline

DATE	ACTIVITY	RESOURCES/DETAILS
1987–1994	Journaling in Ohio at OSU. Creative writing, including autobiographical essay at Valencia Community College in Florida taught by Linda Goddard, MA Read memoirs and books about how to write memoir. Wrote autobiographical essays at Rollins College in Florida for memoir classes with Dr. Lezlie Laws.	1. *Composing a Life* by Mary Catherine Bateson 2. *Your Life as Story* by Tristine Rainer 3. *The Scene Book: A Primer for the Fiction Writer* by Sandra Scofield 4. *Writing the Memoir: From Truth to Art* by Judith Barrington 5. *Self-Editing for Fiction Writers* by Browne & King 6. *The Art of Subtext* by Charles Baxter
1991	Journal entry about The Way written for a course at Rollins College called "Expository Writing: Literature" taught by Dr. Lezlie Laws.	On the journal entry, Dr. Laws wrote a note suggesting that I "write this up into something."
2002	Submitted "An Affinity for Windows," a short memoir based on the 1991 journal entry featuring my Way experience.	Dr. Laws announces anthology project. Asks Rollins's women students to submit stories of their transformations in the classroom.
2004	The short memoir "An Affinity for Windows" was published in: *Shifting Gears: Small, Startling Moments In and Out of the Classroom, 21 Stories by Women of Rollins College*.	Red Pepper Press. Winter Park, FL. Editors: Karen Love Blumenthal, Mary Ann de Stefano, Juliet Weller Dunsworth, Wendy White Goddard, Dr. Lezlie Laws. Limited printing. No ISBN.
2004	Decision to write a book expanding the story in "An Affinity for Windows."	Kept reading, writing. Read memoirs. Did more research using Way magazines, old notes, letters, journals, calendars, and photographs.

Appendix 1: Timeline   219

DATE	ACTIVITY	RESOURCES/DETAILS
2005	Negotiated four-day work week at the software company where I worked full time. Did that for about four months, then returned to full-time; laid aside the book project.	Kept reading, writing.
2007	Retired from career as technical writer and proposal writer in software industry to write my memoir about The Way.	Kept reading, writing. Read books on cults, fundamentalism, the writing process, and read many other memoirs. One favorite: *The Tender Bar* by J. R. Moehringer.
2012	Hired editor Mary Ann de Stefano, owner of MAD About Words, for first professional evaluation/edit of the manuscript. Title: *Nothing But The Word* **246,882 words (728 pgs)**	I read *Crazy for God*, a memoir by Frank Schaeffer whose parents helped found The Religious Right and formed the L'Abri mission in Switzerland that I mentioned in my book. In 1970, I considered going there. Decided to ask Frank to read and blurb my memoir when the time came.
2012–2014	Made major revisions.	Solicited feedback from "beta" readers. Learned to write better dialog. Found help in Chapter 6 of *Self-Editing for Fiction Writers* by Browne & King.
Jan. 12, 2015	Hired another editor for a second professional structural edit of the manuscript. Title: *One Who Got Away: A Memoir of 17 Years in a Bible Cult* **139,990 words (457 pages)** Cut 6,892 words since 2012 version.	Alice Peck Editorial in Brooklyn, NY.

DATE	ACTIVITY	RESOURCES/DETAILS
Feb. 2015– May 2015	Made structural changes per editor, Alice Peck.	E.g.: Used a different chapter for the first chapter. Cut extraneous material.
Spring– Fall 2015	Fifteen sessions of reading the manuscript aloud to my former memoir teacher: Dr. Lezlie Laws, Emeritus Professor of English, Rollins College.	Per feedback, made edits to clarify bits of story.
Summer 2015	Obtained feedback from "beta" readers.	I asked for responses to specific parts of the story.
Spring 2015– Winter 2016	Submitted to agents, small publishing houses, e.g.: Beacon Press.	Collected rejections.
March 2016	Decided to self-publish. Bought a book about how to do it.	*The Complete Guide to Self-Publishing* by Marilyn Ross & Sue Collier.
March 2016	Changed title to: *Undertow: My Escape from the Fundamentalism and Cult Control of The Way International*.	Subtitle has "focus" words for Internet searchability. My husband, Hoyt, and I decided on the title together.
March 2016	Hired book designer (interviewed three).	Duane Stapp, Brooklyn, NY.
March 2016	Hired copy/line editor (interviewed four).	Ruth Mullen, Riverdale, NY.

Appendix 1: Timeline

DATE	ACTIVITY	RESOURCES/DETAILS
April–June 2016	Incorporated more feedback from "beta" readers.	Fact-checking done with former Way members, family members, old friends.
May 2016	Established New Wings Press, LLC. Solicited other authors and experts to read manuscript and write endorsements.	Deadline for blurbs: October 1, 2016. Frank Schaeffer read *Undertow* and sent a blurb. I put a portion of it on front cover.
June 13, 2016	Copy/line editor began work.	Ruth Mullen, Riverdale, NY.
August 2016	Professional author photograph done.	Scott Cook, Orlando, FL.
Sept. 2016	Copy editor, Ruth, finished her work. I sent Duane, the book designer, finalized manuscript of *Undertow* to lay out.	Teamwork pays off!
Oct. 2016	Blurbs were sent to me. Book designer, Duane, finished layout. I did final proofreading of his layout.	I made changes, Ruth double-checked all blurbs, copyright page, author bio. I bought ISBN number, barcode, etc. Book designer, Duane, added these items. Ruth edited back cover.
Oct. 2016	Sent manuscript in PDF to Library of Congress to get a Control Number. Took about a week.	Duane added number to copyright page.

DATE	ACTIVITY	RESOURCES/DETAILS
Nov. 21, 2016	Self-published using IngramSpark, a print-on-demand company & distributor. https://www.ingramspark.com Title: *Undertow: My Escape from the Fundamentalism and Cult Control of The Way International* **Approx. 105,835 words** Cut 34,155 words from 2015 version. 448 pages, incl. front pages, Notes, Bibliography, Acknowledgments, 33 photographs.	Met goal of publishing before the anniversary of my mother's death in 1968, the day before Thanksgiving. Trade secret from *The Complete Guide to Self-Publishing*: Books published after September 15 of any year can carry the next year's copyright date. That's why *Undertow* has the copyright year of 2017.

Appendix 2

MINI-MARKETING FLYER

The following is the content for the marketing flyer I refer to in the essay "Mini-Marketing for Maxi-Messages," in this guidebook. To make one for your book: open a Word document, select Layout, Orientation, Landscape, then select Columns, Two. If you use the same amount of text as I did below, it'll fit into each column. Result: two copies of the flyer from one 8½" x 11" page cut in half.

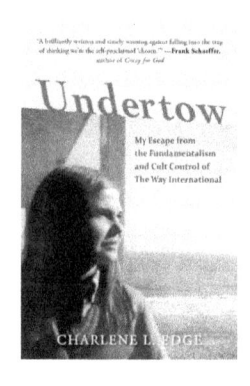

Undertow: **My Escape from the Fundamentalism and Cult Control of The Way International**

by Charlene L. Edge. Memoir.
Paperback and eBook at major booksellers & indie bookstores

"… A frank, in-depth account of one woman's struggles in a controlling organization."
—*Kirkus Reviews*

Gold medal winner – Florida Authors and Publishers Association, 2017.

On Book Riot's list of "100 Must-Read Books About Life in Cults and Oppressive Religious Sects."

What it's about: After a family tragedy struck, teenaged Charlene rejected Catholicism, family, and friends to join what became one of the largest fundamentalist cults in America: The Way International led by Victor Paul Wierwille. After promotion to the inner circle of biblical researchers, Charlene discovered secrets: Wierwille's plagiarism, misuse of Scripture, and sex abuse. Amid chaos at The Way's headquarters, Charlene escaped.

Why *Undertow* matters: Each year about 50,000 to 100,000 people enter or leave high-control groups called "cults" (data: The International Cultic Studies Association). Movies like *Going Clear* and *The Path* have captured the nation's attention. *Undertow* is a personal story about cult recruitment and fear-based manipulation by an authoritarian, charismatic leader. The fundamentalist mindset, espousing certainty about God and the meaning of the Bible, causes untold divisions in families and communities. *Undertow* shows this pain from an insider's perspective and that healing is possible.

A taste of *Undertow*: "I gulped down Doug's words without doing any critical thinking, not pressing him to prove what he said. He was so sincere that I clung to his assertions, like 'believing equals receiving,' as if they were heaven-sent."

CHARLENE L. EDGE spent 17 years in The Way (1970–1987). Later she earned a BA in English from Rollins College and worked for more than a decade as a writer in the software industry. She is a published poet and essayist and a member of the Florida Writers Association, the Authors Guild, and the International Cultic Studies Association. She lives in Florida with her husband, Dr. Hoyt L. Edge and blogs at: http://charleneedge.com.

SELECTED BIBLIOGRAPHY

Note: The following are works cited in this book, *From the Porch to the Page: A Guidebook for the Writing Life*. Additional books for recommended reading are listed at the end of some sections in this book. Important to know: I have not and will not receive financial remuneration to mention any other writer's books, poems, articles, or other material in this guidebook.

Arana, Marie, ed. *The Writing Life: Writers on How They Think and Work*. New York: PublicAffairs, 2003.

Atwood, Margaret. *The Handmaid's Tale*. New York: Anchor Books, 1986.

Barrington, Judith. *Writing the Memoir: From Truth to Art*. Portland, OR: Eighth Mountain, 2002.

Browne, Renni, and Dave King. *Self-Editing for Fiction Writers: How to Edit Yourself into Print*. 2nd ed. New York: HarperCollins, 2004.

Camus, Albert. *The Plague*. Translated by Stuart Gilbert. New York: Vintage, 1991. Originally published as *La peste* (France: Éditions Gallimard, 1947).

Cheney, Theodore A. Rees. *Getting the Words Right, Second Edition: 39 Ways to Improve Your Writing*. Cincinnati: Writer's Digest Books, 2005.

Deutsch, Laura. "Is It Better to Write by Hand or Computer?" *Psychology Today,* October 2, 2017, https://www.psychologytoday.com/us/blog/memory-catcher/201710/is-it-better-write-hand-or-computer.

Dillard, Annie. *The Writing Life*. New York: Harper & Row, 1989.

———. *Pilgrim at Tinker Creek*. New York: Harper & Row, 1974.

Dubus II, Andre. "First Books." In *Meditations from a Movable Chair*. New York: Vintage Books, 1998.

Fish, Stanley. *How to Write a Sentence: And How to Read One*. New York: HarperCollins, 2011.

Gendler, J. Ruth. *The Book of Qualities*. Berkeley: Turquoise Mountain, 1984.

Heffron, Jack. *The Writer's Idea Book: How to Develop Great Ideas for Fiction, Nonfiction, Poetry, & Screenplays*. Cincinnati: Writer's Digest Books, 2000.

Herbert, George. "The Church Porch" poem at https://www.quotes.net/quote/58224. *(For a biography of Herbert, visit* https://www.poetryfoundation.org/poets/george-herbert.*)*

Hesse, Hermann. *Steppenwolf.* New York: Holt, Rinehart and Winston, 1963.

Hyde, Lewis. *The Gift: Imagination and the Erotic Life of Property.* New York: Vintage Books, 1983.

Johnson, Robert. *Inner Work: Using Dreams and Active Imagination for Personal Growth.* New York: HarperCollins, 1986.

Junod, Tom. "What Would Mr. Rogers Do?" *Atlantic Magazine*, December 2019.

Keller, Gary, with Jay Papasan. *The ONE Thing: The Surprisingly Simple Truth Behind Extraordinary Results.* Austin: Bard Press, 2012.

King, Stephen. *On Writing: A Memoir of the Craft.* New York: Scribner, 2000.

Lakoff, George, and Mark Johnson. *Metaphors We Live By.* Chicago: University of Chicago Press, 1980.

Lamott, Anne. *Bird by Bird: Some Instructions on Writing and Life.* New York: Pantheon Books, 1994.

Landon, Brooks. *Building Great Sentences: Exploring the Writer's Craft.* Lecture Transcript and Course Guidebook (Part 1 of 2) in *The Great Courses: Teaching That Engages the Mind.* Chantilly, Virginia: The Teaching Company, 2008.

Lopez, Barry. *Resistance.* Colorado Springs: Waterbrook Press, 2005.

Ondaatje, Michael. *The English Patient.* New York: Vintage International, 1992.

Polking, Kirk, ed. *Beginning Writer's Answer Book*. Cincinnati: Writers Digest Books, 1993.

Shakespeare, William. *Hamlet*. Included in *The Harvard Classics: Elizabethan Drama: Marlowe, Shakespeare*, ed. Charles W. Eliot, LL.D., New York: P. F. Collier & Son, 1938.

Shapard, Robert, and James Thomas, eds. *Sudden Fiction: American Short Stories*. Layton, UT: Peregrine Smith Books, 1986.

Sontag, Susan. *As Consciousness Is Harnessed to Flesh: Journals and Notebooks, 1964-1980*. David Rieff, ed. New York: Picador, 2012.

Sullivan, James. *Over the Moat: Love Among the Ruins of Imperial Vietnam*. New York: St. Martin's Press, 2004.

Sussman, Aaron, and Ruth Goode. *The Magic of Walking*. New York: Simon & Schuster, 1967.

Tan, Amy. *The Opposite of Fate: Memories of a Writing Life*. New York: Penguin Books, 2003.

Thoreau, Henry David and Bob Blaisdell. *Thoreau: A Book of Quotations*. North Chelmsford, MA: Courier, 2011.

Ueland, Brenda. *If You Want to Write: A Book about Art, Independence and Spirit*. Saint Paul: Graywolf Press, 1987.

———. *ME: A Memoir*. New York: Duluth, MN: Holy Cow! Press, 1994. (*For a short biography of Ueland, visit* https://www.goodreads.com/author/show/145456.Brenda_Ueland.)

Whyte, David. *Consolations: The Solace, Nourishment and Underlying Meaning of Everyday Words*. Langley, WA: Many Rivers Press, 2015.

Williams, William Carlos. *Asphodel, That Greeny Flower & Other Love Poems*. New York: New Directions, 1994.

Woolf, Virginia. *Moments of Being*. Orlando, FL: Harcourt Brace Jovanovich, 1985.

Zinsser, William. *On Writing Well: An Informal Guide to Writing Nonfiction.* New York: HarperCollins, 1990.

ABOUT THE AUTHOR

Charlene Edge's most recent book is *From the Porch to the Page: A Guidebook for the Writing Life*—a delightful multi-genre collection with something for every reader and writer.

She is also the author of the award-winning memoir, *Undertow: My Escape from the Fundamentalism and Cult Control of The Way International.*

Charlene grew up on the Eastern Shore of Maryland in a Roman Catholic family. In college, students recruited her into The Way International, a Bible-based cult; she gave it the next seventeen years of her life. After escaping The Way in 1987, she earned a BA in English Literature from Rollins College, graduating *summa cum laude,* and worked for more than a decade as a technical writer and proposal writer in the software industry.

She is a published short-short story writer, an award-winning poet, and a member of the Florida Writers Association, The Authors Guild, and the International Cultic Studies Association.

Charlene lives in Florida with her husband, Dr. Hoyt L. Edge, PhD, Professor Emeritus of Philosophy at Rollins College. On her website, she blogs about their world travels, the writing life, fundamentalism, cults, and whatever catches her imagination. She loves to walk, swim, and read as many books as she can. Visit her at https://charleneedge.com. Author photo by Hoyt L. Edge, taken at Rollins College, 2021.

CPSIA information can be obtained
at www.ICGtesting.com
Printed in the USA
LVHW032232050422
714962LV00003B/16